table flowers

table flowers
paula pryke

RIZZOLI
NEW YORK

photography Sarah Cuttle

To all my friends and family who have made sitting round a
table and enjoying their company one of the great joys of life.
Long may we all share tables together! Cheers!

First published in
the United States of America
in 2007 by
Rizzoli International Publications, Inc.
300 Park Avenue South
New York, NY 10010
www.rizzoliusa.com

Originally published in
the United Kingdom in 2007 by
Jacqui Small LLP,
An imprint of Aurum Books Ltd
7 Greenland Street, London NW1 0ND

PUBLISHER Jacqui Small
EDITORIAL MANAGER Kate John
DESIGNER Maggie Town
EDITOR Sian Parkhouse
PRODUCTION Peter Colley

2007 2008 2009 2010 / 10 9 8 7 6 5 4 3 2 1

ISBN: 978-0-8478-2962-0

Library of Congress Control Number:
2007924731

Printed in Singapore

contents

RIGHT One of our most
popular table centers is a
metal frame that holds five
nightlights, with a leaf-covered
bowl placed in the middle.
This summer arrangement
uses white peonies, with
'Margaret Merril,' 'Julia's
Baby,' and 'Vendella' roses,
cream double eustoma, white
sweet pea, *Alchemilla mollis*,
variegated weigela, and
Eucalyptus parvifolia.

introduction

the practice of adorning tables with flowers, herbs, and petals dates
as far back as ancient Greece and Rome and has endured to the present day. Flower arranging is
an art form that enhances the quality of life, and anyone who loves flowers wants to be able to
arrange them more effectively and creatively. Once this was just the preserve of the rich, but
nowadays the purchase of a bunch of flowers has very much become part of life. The growth
of the flower industry and the widespread road and air freight of this once fragile commodity
means that inexpensive flowers are now available throughout the year.

This book sets out to help, inspire, and teach flower lovers how to create lovely
centerpieces for their tables and decorations for their homes. The intent of this book is to provide
information that opens the door to flower arranging for the novice, and also to offer creative and
imaginative ideas to the more experienced flower arranger. For many in my industry, this book—
like many of my others—will be a useful starting point for a discussion with a client and may
possibly be used as a portfolio of designs. For those planning a celebration, it will be a valuable
source on seasonal availability and also present many diverse ways to deck your tables!

Many of my favorite, tried-and-tested table designs use the same containers, so throughout
the book you will see some of my favorites reappear. Often these containers are not really vases, but

are other items that I have found to be extremely versatile over the years. One of my favorite sections involves taking one vase and filling it differently throughout the seasons. Hopefully, this book will inspire you to use glass containers more diversely and also give you some tips on what kind of containers flowers work best in. As well as showcasing some new designs, this book also details all my favorite classic styles that endure over the years. The flower varieties and the foliage may change, but the overall look remains very similar—classical flower arrangements work well in modern as well as more traditional venues.

Traditional flower arranging books have for a long time started with a list of arrangements and a discussion of the style and shapes of arrangements with no particular reference to where they might be placed. Many of these shapes and styles have no particular relevance to everyday flower arranging or even modern floral design, so, for the purposes of this book, we have only included arrangements that are popular and contemporary. As a florist, I nearly always take cues for an arrangement from the location where the flowers will eventually be placed, and it seems therefore that, as the vast majority end up on tables, this is a good place to start. Enjoy!

choosing your flowers

1 **Zantedeschia** Funnel-shaped arum or calla lily, available in a number of eye-catching colors. Useful for minimal and wedding designs, but look fantastic massed together when you are feeling extravagant!

2 **Tulip** Small waxy spring flower in a huge choice of colors and varieties, including fringed and parrot. Good for hand-tied bouquets and vase arrangements.

3 **Eustoma** Delicate bell-shaped, all-year-round flowers, previously known as lisianthus. Give movement to arrangements and hand-tied bouquets.

4 **Gerbera** Fun, daisy-shaped flower available in an immense choice of colors and in two sizes. Gerberas are very versatile and are suitable for all aspects of floristry.

5 **Papaver** Delicate, cup-shaped flower with papery petals in a wide array of colors. Suitable for architectural vase arrangements, massed and textural work.

6 **Hyacinth** Heavy spikes of waxy bell-shaped fragrant spring flowers in white, blue, pink, purple, cream, or red that are great for hand-tieds. The bells are perfect for piping and wiring to tie a napkin.

7 **Anemone** Shallow cup-shaped spring flower in shades of jewel-like colors. Best in hand-tieds and vases as they are thirsty.

8 **Narcissus** Elegant spring flowers, in yellow or white. Great for vase arrangements, hand-tied bouquets, and small posies.

9 **Gloriosa lily** This stunning two-tone flower is available in long lengths and short stems, perfect for use on its own or as a muse for pink, yellow, and lime table centers.

10 **Sunflower** Flowers with golden-yellow petals radiating from a large, dark center. Best displayed on their own in vases or in large arrangements.

florists' favorites

living and working so close to the huge Dutch auctions in the Netherlands means that I am completely spoiled for choice when it comes to cut flowers. We visit our local market in London where we purchase around 50 percent of our flowers and foliage daily. We buy a lot of Dutch flowers, our favorite Italian varieties, and some local English flowers (which are sadly diminishing) there. Boxes of South American flowers come to us direct, and we have one or two other local specialized suppliers, but mostly our supply either comes through the huge Dutch auctions or is grown there and delivered to the door by huge trucks. There are lots of flowers and choice available throughout the year, and provided budget is not a huge consideration, you can have pretty much what you want when you need it. There are still some

seasonal flowers, I am delighted to say, because if everything were available all year round, it would devalue the product. We can all see how this has been achieved with carnations and chrysanthemums. Within these two huge flower groups there are lots of spectacularly beautiful varieties, but their very ubiquity has lost them some of their cachet. Some flowers manage to become year-round flowers without losing their popularity, such as lily-of-the-valley, which is grown under cold frame, throughout the year for weddings. As there is only a limited supply and the price is prohibitive, it maintains its status and is still an absolute seasonal delight in late April and early May when it comes into its rightful season.

I guess I probably have around 500 varieties of flower that I really love (although I can find some beauty in all flowers), and these favorites come up year after year on my specification lists. My suppliers know which are the ones we adore as a company, and they are always on the lookout for something new for us to try. In my own home I like to use expensive long-lasting flowers as I get better value for my time, but my heart is really taken by the very short-lived and usually scented flower such as sweet peas, stocks, and jasmine.

ABOVE An autumnal round hand-tied bouquet of 'Grand Prix' roses, burgundy ranunculus, and purple anemones mixed with skimmia is arranged in a glass cylinder filled with cranberries.
RIGHT A clashing combination of bright pinks and oranges for a Bat Mitzvah table decoration: Small orange 'Mistique' and 'Malibu' Germini gerberas are mixed with orange marigolds, astrantia, berried ivy, skimmia, and 'Amalia' and 'Prima Donna' roses.
OPPOSITE This low table arrangement gets its vibrant color from an exotic selection of leucospermums, viburnum berries, cotinus, celosia, pink Germini gerberas, gloriosa, and 'Milano,' 'Orange Juice,' 'Wow,' and 'Supergreen' roses.

❶ Rose An astonishing array of colors, sizes, and shapes, makes roses the most popular flower in the floristry industry.

❷ Scabious Open, ruffled flowers in blue, mauve, crimson, or white, this summer flower looks stunning in hand-tied bouquets, giving a "country garden" feel.

❸ Cosmos Graceful, disk-shaped flowers in pink, white, and red. Chocolate cosmos is a striking bridal flower, with the subtle aroma of its namesake.

❹ Zinnia Large, daisy-shaped dazzling flowers that give a retro and fun feel to hand-tied bouquets and vase arrangements.

❺ Sweet Pea Delicate, fragrant flowers on very slender stems, sweet peas come in a wide variety of colors. Good for simple vase arrangements and popular for weddings.

❻ Hellebore Cup-shaped, white, green, or purple flowers, some with unusual speckled markings. Suitable for simple glass vase arrangements and small posies.

❼ Chrysanthemum Long-lasting blooms, available in many different colors and a wide range of shapes and sizes. Chrysanthemums are very versatile flowers and are suitable for all floristry uses.

❽ Dahlia Long-stemmed summer flowers in a range of colors, shapes, and sizes. Add a textual interest to hand-tied bouquets and vase arrangements.

❾ Hydrangea Large, long-lasting flowers appear in white, pink, or blue, turning brown-red in the fall. Look stunning en masse, in grouped bouquets, and a good choice for pedestals.

❿ Lilac Large trusses of flowers in varying shades of purple through to white. Beautiful, versatile, and often scented, lilacs are ideal for hand-tied bouquets.

garden favorites

the distinction between garden and florist flowers for the high-end florist is now rather more blurred than it was a few decades ago. Traditionally, small nurseries and specialized growers produced low quantities of flowers that were sent to the nearest wholesale market. Over the years, many of these small nurseries struggled to make a living producing something they loved. Having traveled around the world seeing flower markets, I have marveled over their rare blooms, but these specialized growers are fading. In the London flower market at Nine Elms Lane, you have to search hard to find rarer flowers, mostly still grown in the Scilly Isles and Cornwall. In San Francisco you meet Italian immigrants who, because they loved the violets of their native home, started nurseries producing this rare and short-lived seasonal product.

LEFT A hand-tied bunch of margarita daisies that could have come fresh from the garden are simply arranged in a terra-cotta pot that has been given an antiqued finish.

BELOW A seasonal arrangement of late summer roses mixed with *Alchemilla mollis*, berried ivy, and hydrangea flowers. Decorative aluminum wire is coiled in the base of the vase to give extra interest.

RIGHT Earthenware jars are filled with hand-tied bouquets of eryngium, margarita daisies, achillea, white commercially grown *Scabiosa caucasiea* var. *alba* with the wild *Scabiosa columbaria* and wild knapweed and fresh green wheat, alongside artichokes hollowed out to hold pillar candles.

Nowadays the constant demand for the unfamiliar and new has meant that many traditional garden flowers have come into mainstream wholesale production. They maintain their seasonality, but are available in quite large numbers. Most of these go through the huge auctions in the Netherlands, but some of them are sold on the Internet. The widespread growth of farmers' and organic markets has also revitalized small growers, and you can get lovely seasonal bunches of flowers if you get there early!

The main difference between garden and commercial flowers is mostly in their longevity. This is partly genetic, in that most heavily hybridized flowers have been selected from stock with excellent vase life. The other major factor is that most commercially grown flowers will be heavily sprayed and be subject to postharvest treatment to ensure their suitability for the long outward journey to their end supplier. Commercially grown sweet peas will be more standard in their appearance and will last possibly five days longer than their casually curly and scented seasonal relatives. The flower market is a huge commercial concern, and once the supermarkets decided to turn their attention to cut flowers, the demand for longer-lasting flowers and the methods by which that is achieved have been increased.

CHOOSING YOUR FLOWERS

❶ **Viburnum** Blue-tinged berries from the viburnum family add depth to arrangements. This heavily berried branch of *Viburnum denatum* is the variety grown commercially in the Netherlands, and is called 'Inge.'

❷ **Pussy willow** Stems are very malleable in the spring and are ideal to cut and line glass containers horizontally. You can line vertically for added interest.

❸ **Guelder rose** Spring flowering foliage, whose zingy acid tone freshens and lifts the effect of adjacent flowers and foliage colors in arrangements.

❹ **Cotinus** Rich dark foliage, which adds depth to arrangements and helps balance bright flower combinations. It also works well with dark reds and burgundy.

❺ **Rose hips** Autumn berries that bring texture and a seasonal feel. Add interest by creating a collar around a cylindrical vase.

❻ **Snowberry** With small pink or white waxy berries, this unusual foliage adds shape and texture to arrangements and is fantastic for wedding arrangements.

❼ **Hypericum** Shiny berries that add texture and interest, varying in color from brown, green, red, and yellow to orange.

❽ **Oak** Rusty brown fall foliage that mixes well with burgundy, brown, plum, and red flowers in arrangements. *Quercus palustris* and *Quercus rubra* are popular.

❾ *Alchemilla mollis* Delicate, lacy lime-green foliage with feathery flowers, ideal for adding a shot of lime to brighten and lift adjacent flower colors.

❿ **Beech** Deep rust-colored fall foliage that mixes well with a host of bright orange flowers and fruits for a sensational seasonal arrangement.

❶

favorite foliage

having always been a huge fan, I love to make arrangements using only a selection of great foliages. Flower arranging in Britain has its origins in the flower gardeners working on large country estates, so our tradition has always been to use a lot of deciduous and evergreen foliage. When I first learned floristry at the Constance Spry School in the late 1980's, the use of foliage was essential for creating natural-looking arrangements. You were taught to learn from nature and take your lead from your plant material. This still forms the basis of many of our arrangements, with the choice of foliage being almost more important than the choice of flowers. For most of my designs, a third of the material would come under the broad heading of foliage.

LEFT A silver cube vase is filled with *Brachyglottis* 'Sunshine' *Alchemilla mollis*, and *Viburnum tinus* foliage to set off the ranunculus, 'Carpe Diem' and 'Renate' roses, and cream 'Grazia' spray roses.
RIGHT A richly toned occasional table arrangement of 'Black Baccara' roses, burgundy carnations, *Viburnum tinus* flowers, black *Capsicum annuum* 'Black Giant'chilies and black-dyed American oak leaves offers sumptuous color offset by lush texture.

In the last 20 years, the growth in foliage varieties commercially available worldwide has been enormous. I feel that this defines the contemporary look. There are currently a lot more seasonal foliages available, and newcomers include *Panicum*. Grasses that are popular in the garden are also all the rage in flower arrangements, giving life and lightness to flowers. Berries are also very important and not just in fall, so certain varieties that started out as seasonal products such as *Hypericum* have now become a year-round staple, available now in more than thirty different varieties pretty much throughout the year. Large leaves such as the *Monstera* were once only found on huge plants, and the cheese plant (so-called because of the natural serrations in its leaves) was really popular—everyone had one in their home. Now you are far more likely to receive a tied bunch edged with one, or see them tucked inside the vase as a part of the overall design style. The new foliage has also extended into the edible area, with herbs being a huge growth area and also branches of *Capsicum* such as the black-fruited *Capsicum annuum* 'Black Giant.' Small sprigs of *Pistacia* make great foliage for a table center, and branches of the apple and the maize family make great vase arrangements for side tables. The use of bare twigs for constructions has given European floristy its own unique style, as well as the use of vines both alive and dried.

celebrating the seasons

BELOW A straight-sided glass bowl was lined with stems of pussy willow, then floral foam was placed in the center and filled with a selection of fresh spring flowers and foliage: *Brachyglottis* 'Sunshine,' *Viburnum opulus*, ranunculus, anemones, and white roses. RIGHT Nestled between the anemone and the *Brachyglottis* 'Sunshine' is a fringed tulip.

spring

Every spring feels like a new beginning to me, and I am always surprised by the arrival of long-forgotten bulbs in the frozen earth. Spring seems like a reward for the cold winter months and a chance to start over again with new resolutions and plans. There are many fragrant flowers at this time of year and the joy of opening the first box of *Narcissus* 'Erlicheer' beats any perfume found inside a bottle.

LEFT In this elegant side-table arrangement, early spring branches, the leafless *Salix* and sprouting forsythia, are used as a frame for calla lilies, poppies, and mimosa. The base has been filled with berried ivy, mimosa, and guelder rose.
RIGHT Branches of simple magnolia make a frame for long-stemmed tulips, with a collar of white lilac.
BELOW RIGHT Giant-headed Clooney ranunculus are arranged in a low square bowl in floral foam covered with green sand, edged with a tied frame of pussy willow.

PREVIOUS PAGES An Easter buffet table arrangement was created using small 'Tête-à-tête' daffodils, muscari, and primrose plants around a beautiful cake by Eric Lanlard.

fresh colors

In my garden, the snowdrops and the hellebores are closely followed by pink fluffy camellias, the widow iris, and then masses of faithful narcissus bulbs. By the time they are over, there is so much stirring in the garden that you know the longer lighter days and better climate are going to entice you outside and into the garden. For florists, the spring selection of flowers really now begins around November, when tulips, ranunculus, anemones, and even poppies start to appear. The woody stems of lilac and guelder roses first appear in our Christmas arrangements, before they find themselves in the more pastel hues of spring.

As an avid lover of color, I tend only to use white in the winter and the spring. There are so many wonderful white flowers in the spring that this is simply my favorite time to use ranunculus, tulips, and anemones with soft silver gray foliages, and the lime green of the guelder rose and the hellebores makes a perfect accompaniment to summer ivories and pastels. Nature itself is a great teacher, and we find ourselves naturally drawn to the dominant colors of the season. Pale yellow can be found in the primroses and narcissus and also on the pollen coming through on catkins and pussy willow. I also love the pale yellow of spring poppies and frilly-edged early tulips.

More than any other time of year, I find myself bringing plants inside for decoration, and more often these will be bulb plants. Easy to grow and look after, they are relatively inexpensive and make beautiful dependable natural decorations for the table. Spring time is also a great time of year to force early branches inside and to create more structural designs, making special use of the ones without leaves and the early signs of spring. My favorites are *Prunus* varieties, but I also love the gnarled and twisted appearance of Japanese magnolia when the buds are still gray but show the promise of their perfect tulip-shaped flowers.

LEFT The abundance of plant material in the summer makes tackling an ambitious design such as this a little less expensive. Try to choose large heads so your flowers will cover the shape fairly quickly— if you use small-headed flowers, you may be surprised to find just how long a design like this may take to produce! I have chosen hydrangea, peonies, and 'Vendella' and 'Popov' roses, and filled in with soft fragrant flowers such as sweet peas, philadelphus, and phlox. The base of this cone-shaped topiary is soaked green floral foam covered with chicken wire anchored in a verdigris urn.

RIGHT The quintessentially beautiful early summer flower. This blown peony 'Coral Charm' nestles among *Viburnum opulus* berries and roses.

summer

Summer is simply the best time for flower arranging. Flowers are plentiful and inexpensive, fruit and vegetables abound, and warm weather presents more opportunity for outdoor dining and special events. Higher light levels encourage you to use more vivid color palettes and lush combinations, but the lime greens of the garden are a perfect backdrop for ivories and whites, too.

LEFT Mixed colored roses, simply arranged in groups in little colored glass votives, make a colorful arrangement for a casual summer party. RIGHT A wooden and metal urn makes a more formal arrangement when filled with midsummer flowers. *Brachyglottis* 'Sunshine' and *Alchemilla mollis* are combined with hydrangea, sweet pea, astilbe, nigella, and roses.

PREVIOUS PAGES A beautiful summer wedding bride's table is decorated with a garland of stephanotis, a cascade of petals, and urns filled with late summer roses, green hydrangea, green *Zinnia* 'Envy,' *Viburnum opulus* berries, and fluffy sprigs of *Cotinus*, or smoke bush.

spoiled for choice

Summer, with its abundance, is usually the flower-lovers' favorite season and it often gives us the most choice of plant material and opportunity for entertaining outdoors. The start of the summer season in the United Kingdom is the Chelsea Flower Show, which is always around the last week in May, when the bluebells in the woods give way to the purple spires of wild foxgloves. I know that I am just about to enjoy the best period in my own garden and also at the flower auctions as lots of my favorite flowers come into their season. During this time there is a profusion of flowers in my favorite palette of pinks and lilacs in varieties such as peonies, sweet peas, and delphinium mixed with blossom such as philadelphus and Solomon's seal to choose from.

The composition of an arrangement is determined by the characteristics of the flowers, and in midsummer, on the one hand, there are lots of lovely large-headed and long-stemmed flowers that are perfect for big arrangements and also lots of very delicate flowers that are perfect for smaller arrangements. Tall lilies, delphiniums, hydrangea, and large-headed peonies look beautiful in huge displays. Conversely, large heads of peonies and hydrangea are great for creating dramatic textural arrangements, either as accents to summer topiaries or as background in an arrangement with other accent flowers such as roses.

Many of the prettiest summer flowers, such as zinnias, astrantia, and nigella, have small delicate round heads on thin or hollow stems. These flowers are best arranged in water unless they are used in foam for a special occasion. When they are arranged together with other smaller-headed delicate flowers such as sweet peas, the overall effect is very dainty and loose. When using quintessential summer flowers, it is best to match them with seasonal foliages. Delicate *Alchemilla mollis* is perfect, a touch of soft-colored hydrangea will work well, too, and another favorite is *Brachyglottis* 'Sunshine.' This soft downy foliage is particularly useful for the flower arranger. An evergreen, it creates a lovely textural effect and looks good in any season. I also like to use herbs in the summer, and there are now an enormous quantity grown for the flower market. Among my favorites are angelica, dill, eupatorium, fennel, bergamot, oregano, mint, rue, sage, tanacetum, thyme, and, of course, lavender.

LEFT To achieve this perfectly round shape, 'Duett' roses, 'Managua' chrysanthemums, *Viburnum tinus*, and cotoneaster berries have been arranged in a floral foam ball and placed on top of a cylinder vase filled with tiny crab apples.

RIGHT An orange 'Tom Pearce' standard chrysanthemum is flanked by the hips of *Rosa* 'Amazing Fantasy' and the red stems of *Salix babylonica* var. *pekinensis* 'Tortuosa' for an irresistible splash of stunning fall color.

fall

The fall brings a more vibrant palette and also a plethora of seed heads and berries that add to the textural quality of your flower selection. In fact, autumnal plant materials are so significant to contemporary flower arranging that lots are incorporated into the all-year-round selection.

BELOW A mixture of orange roses has been hand tied with amaranthus, hypericum, cotoneaster, and *Euphorbia fulgens* and placed in a round bowl filled with crab apples to make a central display for an autumnal buffet table.

RIGHT A vase of *Photinia* 'Red Robin,' rose hips, and *Physalis*.

OPPOSITE This textural table arrangement has roses and chrysanthemums mixed with orange celosia and seasonal apples. A mix of *Brachyglottis* 'Sunshine,' *Alchemilla mollis*, skimmia, ivy berries, and *Photinia* make it very natural.

PREVIOUS PAGES Hand-tied bouquets of 'Classic Duett,' 'Dance Ballet,' 'Renate,' and 'Toucan' roses are set in low bowls filled with crab apples. Autumnal leaves line red votives and mulberry twigs with wild clematis and sprigs of crab apples garland the table. Mulberry twigs are also tied around the napkins.

color power

I am particularly fond of the fall palette because it shifts to dark red, burgundy, purples, ochres, and browns, and the intensity of color and diversity of sculptural material makes for exciting combinations. The autumn flowers I enjoy working with are dahlias, chocolate cosmos, spindle berries, and callicarpa, and clusters of deep purple fall fruits such as elderflower berries, damsons, and spiky sloes. The darkest black berries from the viburnum, and ligustrum berries mixed with spiky trails of blackberries make a rich contrast to some of the brighter flowers of the season, such as nerines, sunflowers, heleniums, and chrysanthemums.

Further into the fall season, the turning foliages mixed with fiery oranges and reds become more prevalent, as different pumpkin varieties find their ways into grocery stores and markets. Our Italian foliage suppliers use a process involving glycerin to prolong life, and these leaves add diversity to our autumnal arrangements. Much later, the empty branches of dogwood and willow start to fill the gaps of the seasonal flowers at the huge Dutch auctions, and they suggest other ideas for table decorations. A lot of small fruit that does not meet supermarket standards also ends up in the auctions, and these tiny pears and apples along with ornamental crab apples and brassicas give texture to autumnal mixes. Rose hips and skimmia are very popular autumnal fillers. Cosmos, sunflowers, and dahlias look great arranged with kernels of chestnuts on the stems.

winter

For the professional florist, there is still an immense choice of flowers even in the deepest part of winter. In my own home with the heat on, I always want to choose flowers that are going to last well and give me good value. Like a lot of things in life, the more expensive flowers sometimes turn out to be the best value because they are very long lasting, and for me that saves time, too!

LEFT A winter topiary of spruce, skimmia, viburnum berries, and ivy mixed with gilded cones, waxed apples, and heads of *Helleborus* is set into a gilded urn for seasonal effect. All the plant material has been wired into a frame that has been filled with sphagnum moss and covered with chicken wire.

RIGHT The beautiful *Helleborus* x *hybridus* is surrounded by gilded pine cones and richly scented blue pine.

LEFT Varying heights of red glass vases are filled with posies of 'Passion' roses, skimmia, and rose hips.
BELOW Four cube vases of white and 'Black Baccara' roses are tied with black bamboo in a checkerboard.
RIGHT A straight glass bowl is filled with black dogwood, waxed red apples, ranunculus, *Viburnum tinus* berries, fruiting ivy, red 'Grand Prix' roses dyed black, and black dahlias.

exotic blooms
Amaryllis have become one of winter's best-value flowers, lasting easily seven days and sometimes much longer. Cymbidium orchids are also in their best season, and although it seems extravagant to cut these flowers up and use them, they can last nearly three weeks arranged in water. The anthurium genus is also worth considering. Many people are not fond of the vivid red varieties, but there are so many fabulous shades that there is normally one to suit your taste.

For the flower arranger using the garden as a main source of material, the winter is the time to focus on evergreens. It can be very soothing to make a display of mixed greens, and I have a great assortment of colors and textures to choose from. This is about the only time of year I use variegated foliages, and I include groups of variegated holly, ivy, pittosporum, and *Euonymus fortunei* 'Sunset' and even *Elaeagnus pungens* 'Maculata' in winter decorations. My favorite winter foliages are spruce, bay, and rosemary for scent and gray *Brachyglottis* 'Sunshine' mixed with lots of trailing ivies and berries. All these foliages last well and look great wired into topiaries for special entertaining. All you need are a few fruits and seed heads and you have an effective long-lasting arrangement. Often I will replace the flowers while the foliage and fruits last for longer periods.

Commercially we use a lot of gray foliage at this time of year, including scented eucalyptus, and other long-lasting silver foliages from South Africa, such as the silver *Brunia albiflora*. There is also a gray foliage imported from Israel that is known as "kochia" but whose botanical name is *Maireana sedifolia*. This, along with eucalyptus pods, gives great texture to winter wreaths and decorations, along with the many seed heads, natural or painted, that flood the market for the holiday season.

PREVIOUS PAGES Topiary lavender trees in gray ceramic cubes have been sprayed with glitter. Garlands of silvered ivy trails are pinned to the table cloth with pink organza bows with added crystals for a sparkly effect. Mirrored votives are scattered across the table— some are filled with tiny posies of 'Sweet Avalanche' roses and sprigs of *Acacia baileyana* 'Purpurea' and some with silver-sprayed crab apples.

take five containers...

Over the years flower fashions come and go, but certain classic containers look good year after year. Like a little black cocktail dress or a blue blazer, they are always in fashion. On the following pages I show my absolute favorite traditional vases.

an urn

This classic pedestal urn is 7 in (19 cm) high—the perfect height for table flowers—and 11 in (29 cm) wide. The foot lifts the flowers high enough above the table to be noticed above the rims of glasses, but not so tall that guests cannot chat with each other. We use these in metal and in fiberglass. The metal ones are very heavy, which allows us to make weightier arrangements. Add a lick of spray paint, and you have a versatile container that looks good in classical and modern locations.

This summer arrangement is made up of grouped 'Coral Charm' peonies, *Rosa* 'Amalia,' *R.* 'Marrakesh,' and *R.* 'Peppermint' with purple astrantia, *Photinia* 'Red Robin,' and viburnum berries. The urn has been given a stone-effect finish that suits the formality of the arrangement.

This looser, fuller autumnal arrangement is made up of cotoneaster berries, ivy berries, American oak, beech, skimmia, eucalyptus, Chinese lanterns, ornamental kales, and 'Léonidas' roses.

Clementines wired into a mossed topiary frame create a stunning winter centerpiece. The naturally glossy camellia leaves have been wired into the design, and the urn has been gilded to match the reflective shine of the fruit and foliage.

This bright and cheerful spring arrangement of lilac, camellia, *Viburnum opulus*, ivy berries, and *Helleborus foetidus*, with pale cream Clooney ranunculus and scented cream narcissi is augmented by branches of catkin. This verdant display is balanced by the verdigris effect of the urn.

a round
glass vase

This simple glass bowl—12 x 4 in (30 cm by
10 cm)—is just perfect for a centerpiece and can
be used in so many ways. When the budget is
small and the occasion does not warrant a lavish
flower arrangement, it can be used to float a few
flowerheads or candles. Being clear, it can be
filled on the inside with reeds, stems, or
branches or it can be used with other accessories
such as candy when a second container is placed
inside the bowl. There are thousands of ways to
use it—the only limit is your imagination.

LEFT Red dogwood has been arranged around a central block of floral foam standing in the glass vase. A tight dome of 'Cool Water,' 'Black Baccara,' and 'Amalia' roses has been placed in the center and a collar of *Muehlenbeckia* vine arranged around the edge.

THIS PAGE For this spring birthday table arrangement, a low bowl has been placed inside another to create a gap in which to display a selection of multicolored jelly beans. The central container then has been filled with foam and arranged with *Viburnum opulus*, ivy berries, and mixed colored Clooney ranunculus to match the jelly beans and coordinate with the tapered candles.

This summer table center has been created using a bowl within a bowl, and the gap filled with highly colored potpourri. The dyed potpourri colors have been matched by an unusual flower combination of dark red peonies; pink, brown, and lilac roses; yellow achillea; *Tanacetum*; purple sweet peas; variegated weigela; and *Alchemilla mollis*.

For a winter centerpiece a
16-in (42-cm) diameter wreath
frame has been placed around
the 12-in (30-cm) bowl, which
has been filled with water and
floating candles. Groups of
flowers and foliage have been
placed in the wreath: tulips,
lilac, guelder rose, *Brunia
laevis*, and green and white
hellebores.

a terra-cotta pot

The simple shape of a terra-cotta pot works well for outdoor events, but it can be dressed up with spray paint or a length of fabric for more formal celebrations. The advantage of terra-cotta in its raw state is that it is a natural product fashioned from the earth, so it works extremely well with flowers and foliage. It is relatively inexpensive and heavy, so it can contain heavy plant material or taller displays. This pot is 9 in (23 cm) high and 8 in (20 cm) wide, although we often use one a size smaller.

RIGHT This pot was covered with purple chiffon and lined and filled with foam to make a colorful centerpiece. It is filled with 'Tradescant,' 'Talea,' 'Naomi,' and 'Luxor' roses, *Zantedeschia* 'Little Suzy,' *Weigela* 'Chaméléon,' *Astilbe* 'Europa,' and 'Erica' and the seed heads of *Papaver somniferum* 'Hen and Chickens.'

FAR RIGHT A tied bunch of *Hippeastrum* 'Charisma' in a gold-sprayed pot with a topping of cranberries makes a perfect winter living topiary.

THIS PAGE To create a candle centerpiece, foam is placed in a lined terra-cotta pot. Lichen-covered twigs, skimmia, hypericum, eucalyptus, and *Viburnum tinus* berries and flowers and contorted willow have been added, then twenty small-headed 'Akito' roses.

RIGHT A hand-tied bunch of white *Tulipa* 'Honeymoon' and pink *Tulipa* 'Bell Song' with a collar of salix and pussy willow makes a simple spring display.

three glass tumblers

Simple glass tumblers are very useful containers for flowers and one of my favorites for the dining table. I like to dot a number—usually six—down the center of a long table and spread votives around them. You can cover them in double-sided tape and make very inexpensive natural containers, or you can fill their insides to create a different effect. They can be adapted very easily to the season; their heavy glass bottoms make them stable, and they can be easily cleaned and used again and again. I also recycle old jars for this purpose so that with a few pretty leaves I can create a lovely inexpensive container.

ABOVE Bunches of *Narcissus* 'Bridal Crown' have been tied just below the flower heads to create individual living topiaries and then set into glasses embedded in sea shells broken into tiny fragments.

BELOW Double-sided tape was wrapped around the glasses and *Stachys byzantina* leaves were attached and tied with cord. Posies of sweet peas, *Triteleia*, margarita daisies, white nigella, forget-me-nots, and *Origanum* 'Gijsie' have been placed in them.

A single 'Tom Pearce' standard chrysanthemum has been encircled with *Rosa* 'Amazing Fantasy,' *Salix babylonica* var. *pekinensis* 'Tortuosa,' and *Quercus palustris*. Autumnal leaves anchored with double-sided tape and tied with sisal cover the glasses.

White candles anchored with wires are placed in floral foam. Ivy, *Viburnum tinus*, *Ilex* berries, and hypericum were placed to cover the wires, before the 'Black Bacarra' roses and white *Helleborus niger* were added. Glossy laurel leaves tied with red cord wrap around the glasses.

a tall
fluted vase

These tall classically shaped fluted vases are very versatile. You can use them on a console table to create elegant displays, or to make stunning table arrangements for an event. The vase is 33 in (85 cm) high and about 10 in (26 cm) wide at the flared top. They can be a little taller, up to 3 ft (1 m), but for a table, 33 in (85 cm) or lower is perfect because it is imposing enough to make a presence in a large foyer, but not so tall that it bears no relation to the table.

An oasis ball was placed in the top of a black vase, set on a base of red *Skimmia japonica*. Sixty *Rosa* 'Ranuncula' have been tightly packed into the foam and ten stems of red dogwood have been placed in the center of the arrangement to echo the shape of the vase.

A clear glass vase has been
filled with *Prunus* stems and
topped with a generously
sized hand-tied bunch of
Tulipa 'Monarch Parrot.'
More of the *Prunus* stems,
with blossoms just beginning
to show on the bare wood,
have been brought through to
emerge from the top of the
arrangement for more height.

personalizing your table

RIGHT Mantelpieces are lovely spots for flower arrangements because they place the flowers at eye level. Here the pink and green colors of the table center have been matched on the mantel flowers. Often the same flowers can be used, but we specify taller hygrangea and long-stemmed roses for larger arrangements than the table centerpieces, for which the flowers will be cut very short. BELOW A tightly packed dome of thirty *Rosa* 'Sterling Silver' is placed in a clear glass vase to keep distraction to a minimum.

putting it all together

One of the best parts of being a florist is having a say in the look of an entire event. Specifying the linen, china, and flatware to match the floral design is a great pleasure, and it is always lovely to see the whole look of an event, however small or grand, come together. Coordination can be achieved at all levels and on any budget.

dressing the table
Linen and napkins are one of my weaknesses, and I am an avid collector of pretty tablecloths, mats, and linen for my home. I often cannot resist buying decorations for my table when I am traveling, and as I am lucky enough to visit very diverse cultures during the course of my work commitments, I have picked up some very unusual pieces. It might be some lovely paper place cards from Italy or some great Provençal linen from a French market, some fine handmade lace from Madeira, or starched Irish linen. Each nation tends to have an interesting tradition for the decoration of their tables, and this has long been one of my passions.

White and ivory linen normally come as part of the package of an event, and often colored linen is charged as an extra. I like to use white and ivory for white as well as multicolored flowers, because the neutral background gives the flowers more impact. Whether you are planning a grand dinner, a family birthday, or an intimate lunch, you can use a few small details to personalize your table. These can be very small and inexpensive, and simple to construct. Candles and votives are an inexpensive way of making an impact as well as creating great ambient lighting.

LEFT A vibrant selection of late summer flowers, including dahlias, achillea, zinnias, and scabious, is mixed with dill and *Alchemilla mollis*. Individual zinnias have been laid on the napkins. All of the elements—the runner, the vases, the napkins, and the glassware—are brought together by color. RIGHT The patterns and colors of a pretty paper tablecloth and accessories have been brought to life by these cube vases filled with roses, zinnias, and *Alchemilla mollis* for a summer barbecue. BELOW This gorgeous individual chocolate cake was created by Eric Lanlard. The gloriosa and acid yellow ribbon make a suitably sumptuous napkin tie to accompany it.

mixing colors and patterns

jazzing it up
Successful combinations of color and pattern are harder for the novice, but any color can be made to work with another, provided there is right balance. If I am using a patterned tablecloth or the room is very decorative, I will take my lead from the fabric and the interior, enhancing the colors rather than working against them. If the pattern is two-tone or monochromatic, I may use a contrasting color to make the flowers stand out from the interior. Using a colorful runner or a brightly colored paper tablecloth is another inexpensive way to make your table look coordinated. There are brilliant designs in paper now, and some of the best looks I have created in my home have been based on paper napkins. For all the designs on these pages, the flowers were chosen in response to the fabric or paper tablecloths.

strong and vibrant These are my trademark colors, and I like to work with unusual combinations. I often take one bicolor flower as a muse, such as the colorful *Gloriosa* with its pink petals edged in yellow and lime, and use that as my starting point. For even more striking color themes, I use contrasting colors such as blue and yellow, or orange and green.

The intensity of color is the degree of saturation that the color projects. A fully saturated color such as brilliant red is more intense than burgundy or maroon. A pale yellow is nearer to white, whereas a very dark brown is nearer to black. When you are thinking about color intensity, it is always a good idea to imagine it in black and white because that gives you some idea about its saturation, which will ultimately affect how it is perceived by the eye.

Colors are lightened and lifted by the addition of white and muted by the addition of black. For all the arrangements shown on these pages, I took my initial inspiration from the colors in the runners or mats for the design.

When you use strong and vibrant colors, you can either soften or mute them with the use of foliage and heavy groups of color, or you can go without foliage and make the most of its intensity. If I am using a lot of heavy color I most often prefer to take out any white. If I am using mixed roses, I think they look better without any very pale colors. Mixed colored ranunculus and dahlias also look best if the white or cream flowers are removed. You can see from the arrangements on these pages how the white flowers advance to the eye when they are used with massed color.

LEFT For a summer lunch, the graphic design of the place mats has been copied in the flower arrangements by using a random color combination of individual heads of sunflower, 'Grand Prix' rose, margarita daisy, a blown open pink and white 'Cézanne' rose, and a yellow and orange 'Circus' rose. Turquoise aluminum wire keeps the flowers in place.
RIGHT The colors of a striped runner were copied in the flowers of a 3-ft (1-m)long floral foam rack. From the front to back it is constructed from hydrangea, 'Cool Water' roses, cotinus, green sedum, 'Amalia' roses, ivy foliage, echinops, red dahlias, yellow achillea, 'Wow' roses, green hydrangea, blue scabious, 'Peppermint' roses, 'Marie-Claire' roses, hydrangea, 'Cool Water' roses, cotinus, sedum, 'Amalia' roses, ivy foliage, echinops, red dahlias, and yellow achillea.

materials

30 *Rosa* 'Happy'

a selection of highly colored
Mikado sticks

a 5-in (14-cm) glass cube vase

2 blocks of floral foam

a roll of double-sided tape

a length of ribbon

bright and breezy

My mother calls this rose "gaudy" and I think that sums it up perfectly! These highly colored
roses have been developed in the Netherlands, and due to a unique coloring application, each
bloom displays all the colors of the rainbow. The process is a secret, but amazingly the result is
said to be achieved by using natural plant-extract dyes that are absorbed by the flowers as they
grow. They have been trademarked 'Happy,' but they are also known as the rainbow rose.

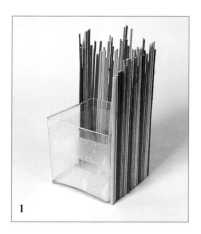

Step 1 Place strips of double-sided
tape around the glass cube vase and
then anchor the highly colored Mikado
sticks around the glass onto the tape,
close together, in stripes of each color.
When the vase is covered, trim the
sticks evenly along the top edge.

Step 2 Soak the floral foam until the
air bubbles cease to rise and then cut it
to fit into the vase so that the foam is at
least ¾ in (2 cm) over the edge of the
container. Trim the roses to 6 in (15 cm)
and remove all leaves from the stems.

Step 3 Begin to create the dome of
roses by placing the first row virtually
horizontally around the top of the sticks.
Continue with the next layer up and then
turn the cube around and work on the
other sides. Complete the dome, taking
care to cover all the green foam. You can
finish off with ribbon if you like.

LEFT A series of single vases displays the eccentric-looking *Allium* 'Schubertii.' The metallic tones of the flower set off the stainless steel table in a very cool-feeling setting.
RIGHT These black and white arrangements consist of dahlias with cotinus and *Daucas carota* 'Dara.'
BELOW A single head of white phalaenopsis orchid placed on a black napkin: nothing tricky here, but the effect is starkly graphic and sophisticated.

creating monotone schemes

keeping it simple
Limited color schemes look very sophisticated, and the use of monochromatic color can be an easy way to create an effective and stylish-looking table. A whole ballroom decked out with just red flowers can be very arresting and yet understated against a mix of vibrant colors. Monochromatic color schemes can use tints or shades or the full intensity of the single color. It is a safe and easy way to plan a theme and usually very popular. My favorites are white, red, and also pink. I am a huge fan of chic black linen and I like the simplicity of black and white, and have designed many parties with that theme even though I love bright colors!

When choosing flowers for these arrangements, it is important to think about textures, variety, and foliage. Color balance is usually achieved through the use of foliage. If you want to tone down the main color, you need to add lots of dark green foliage. If you want to make the color really sing, add more and more lime green to the mix, and the color combinations will be all the more vibrant and shocking.

LEFT A white-painted French wire basket has been filled with *Viburnum opulus*, white lilac, white ranunculus, white bouvardia, white stock, white 'Ice Queen' gerberas, and white tulips. ABOVE A single head of 'Ice Queen' gerbera tops the pyramid-folded napkin.

statement colors

One single dominant color is often the starting point for planning the flowers for a celebration. This may be determined by the interior or the room, the table linen, or simply the personal choice of the host or hostess. The strangest request I ever had was to match the flower to the favorite Chanel nail polish color of the hostess! If the color statement chosen is not a flower color that occurs in nature, such as turquoise or aqua, it is often best to use a contrasting color such as a bright pink or dark red. Black or dark brown work best with stronger colors or light colors than muted colors.

Color needs to be considered when looking at the location and the lighting. Blues and violets recede when viewed from a distance. Oranges and yellows are warm colors and advance so that they are more noticeable. If you want a room to look more intimate, you need to use advancing colors. Artificial lighting drains all the color out of blue flowers, and they work best with natural daylight. For a candlelit venue, pastel colors show up best. Special occasions will also suggest statement colors.

Statement color is also very seasonal: yellow for spring; pink, lilac, and blue for summer; orange, ochre, and brown for fall; and red and white for the holiday season. New color fashions come and go, but nature has a very compelling way of presenting seasonal color throughout the year, and it is very interesting how we react to this.

OPPOSITE A straight glass bowl has been filled with red dogwood, floral foam, then ivy berries and red skimmia followed by 'Naomi' and 'Black Baccara' roses, red Clooney ranunculus, and 'Ronaldo' tulips. Red petals have been scattered on the marble table to extend the display.

materials

10 orange 'Real' gerbera

a bunch of orange dyed *Anemone coronaria*

a bunch of *Viburnum tinus* berries

a bunch of *Hedera helix* berries

a bunch of *Skimmia japonica* 'Rubella'

10 *Rosa* 'Trixx'

12 *Rosa* 'Tropical Amazone'

7 *Rosa* 'Eldorado'

9 *Rosa* 'Apricot'

5 medium-sized oranges

a stemmed glass bowl

a roll of floral tape

a sharp knife

3 blocks of floral foam

orange monotone

Arrangements of one color can be very striking as there is great intensity and saturation. Massed monochromatic flowers are a favorite design style of mine, not least because they look very effective in both informal and formal situations. This is a style I use a lot in my own home so that the flower arrangement adds an accent to an interior.

Step 1 Soak the floral foam in water until bubbles stop rising. Cut the oranges into thin slices and place a layer on the bottom of the bowl. Cut and stack the foam in the glass bowl on top of the first layer of fruit so that it sits at least 2 in (5 cm) above the edge of the container. Use as much foam as you can to fill the bowl because this will save on fruit. Place the rest of the sliced fruit down all the sides of the bowl and then secure the foam in place with floral tape.

Step 2 Green up the arrangement by using the three foliages at different heights and depths in the foam. Keep twisting the bowl around to create a rounded effect. If you work on all sides, you will get a more uniform look. Make sure as you place the stems that they are all angled toward the central point.

Step 3 Add the flowers to the arrangement. Start with the softer stems such as the anemones and gerbera and then fill in with the roses, mixing the varieties as much as possible. To maximize the color I have kept the length of the flowers all the same, which gives a more rounded "massed" effect. Fill up with water and serve!

individual place settings

Using a number of smaller arrangements is a simple way of adding color throughout the table and is great for long or large round tables. I often use individual table settings on long tables to keep the center free for serving and for platters of food from which guests can help themselves.

ABOVE LEFT A bunch of 30 'Honeymoon' tulips have been hand tied and placed in a frosted glass vase. If you ensure the containers are stylish yet not too expensive, you can afford to give away your flower displays to your guests as they leave, if you wish, as a thank you for coming.

ABOVE RIGHT White astilbe, white ranunculus and white hellebores are combined in a silver-rimmed beaker. A pretty arrangment such as this placed next to each setting would be a delightfully personal welcome for your guests, and make them feel really appreciated.

For special events the contemporary trend is to have a number of individual or grouped arrangements on a table. Sometimes these may be used as a gift for each guest or as the favor to which you can attach a name or place card. My favorites are small plants such as herbs, bulbs, and succulents, and I generally choose what is best value and in season. For birthday parties, I often use simple margarita daisies, geraniums, or small compact plants such as mind-your-own-business or orange bead plant. Recently, there has been a rise in the number of miniature novelty plants available, and in particular dainty little orchids are perfect for special occasions or special family get-togethers. For weddings we often tie individual flowers or a small posy of flowers on a napkin or occasionally attach the name of the guest on a single stem of calla lily, peony, or rose.

The individual place setting looks most effective when the color scheme is monochromatic, and I think this kind of flower collection works best with white or soothing colors such as blue. Receding colors are my preference for multiple individual flower arrangements. My exceptions to this would be in the spring when I might use yellow for a party for children or younger people. Simple designs and one-color arrangements look best on long tables.

RIGHT I love bright pink and yellow together, and here yellow dot spray roses have been mixed with bright pink 'Christian' spray roses, standard 'Amalia' roses, and bright yellow achillea. The lime green *Alchemilla mollis* makes the colors even more vibrant, and the matching sand just sets it all off. Star confetti is a cheap and cheerful way to make a table look more festive.

BELOW Flowers and foliage combine in this small table arrangement of *Viburnum opulus* berries, rudbeckia, 'Amalia' roses, and bright green zinnia.
BELOW RIGHT An antiqued terra-cotta pot is filled with a pillar candle wired into floral foam and then surrounded by a collar of mixed roses, bouvardia, and hydrangea.

OPPOSITE An orange ceramic cube is filled with red skimmia, 'Naomi' roses, red Clooney ranunculus, and 'Palomino' roses. The flower heads are packed tightly together to maintain a compact shape.

smaller scale
Flowers that are too delicate or small for grander arrangements come into their own in compact displays. In spring, try miniature daffodils, *Muscari*, and tiny fritillaries; in summer, everlasting sweet peas, small pinks, and nigella; in fall, helenium, zinnias, and delicate nerines are perfect. Smart caterers use flowers and foliage to match so the flowers and food mix in a sensuous way.

Containers 4–5 in (10–12 cm) in height and width are the perfect size. Either use a small amount of foam, keep the flowers very short, or mass a few flowers into a very dense and short hand-tied bouquet. When using candles, always use foam to safely anchor the candle into the center. When space is very tight, use a single bud vase for the center of each table. Generally speaking the size of the arrangement determines the size of the flower head, so more delicate flowers like zinnias and bouvardia should be used rather than large-headed and thick-stemmed or woody flowers. When specifying flowers for delicate arrangements, it is also prudent to pick naturally short-stemmed flowers because they are cheaper and otherwise you are going to end up cutting the flower down enormously.

materials

for the place setting
a small packet of star anise
a 5-in (12-cm) glass cube
a glass tumbler
a small cyclamen plant
Muehlenbeckia vine

for the votive
3 good-sized oranges
a small pack of cloves
3 votive candles
a paring knife

spiced-up cyclamen

Plants make very attractive and simple decorations for tables. They are often overlooked in favor of cut flowers, but I often incorporate small plants and bulbs in my table decorations, particularly in the winter and spring when flowers are more scarce. They also make great inexpensive giveaways after a Sunday lunch or special dinner party.

Step 1 With a sharp paring knife cut away the peel at the top of the orange and carve out some of the flesh so that you can just fit in a votive. Be careful not to overdo it as the candle should fit snugly for a neat finish.

Step 2 Add a ring of cloves around the candle, pressing the stems into the cut edge of the orange peel. Keep them as closely packed as you can.

Step 3 Place the glass tumbler inside the cube vase and fill the gap between them with star anise right up to the top of the vase.

Step 4 Soak the plant well and then remove it from its pot and place it in the central glass. Add a little *Muehlenbeckia* vine over the top to conceal the potting mixture. Arrange the orange votives around the pots at each place setting. When lit, the heat from the candles will accentuate the smell of citrus and cloves.

materials

an aspidistra leaf

a small water phial

a roll of double-sided tape

a length of ribbon

a *Rosa* 'Illusion'

napkin decorations

My publisher Jacqui Small is crazy about napkin details and makes sure we pack as many as possible into every flower book we do! It is certainly an easy way to make a statement and personalize a table, and make a few flowers appear very special to your guests.

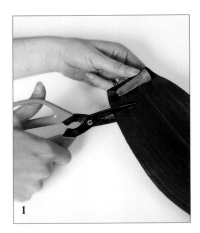

OPPOSITE, TOP LEFT A 'Black Baccara' rose, hypericum, and ivy berries tied by lime-green ribbon. TOP RIGHT A 'Candy Bianca' rose tucked inside a folded napkin. BOTTOM LEFT A 'Julia's Baby' rose tied with an organdy bow. BOTTOM RIGHT A 'Talea' rose with pearlized corsage bracelet.

Step 1 Phials are available for purchase, but we generally recycle ones that come on flowers from the growers. Cover the outside of the phial with double-sided tape, remove the outer paper, and then cut the aspidistra leaf to cover the phial completely.

Step 2 Cut the stem of the rose head to the size you require for your napkin and then place it into the phial.

Step 3 Make a bow by creating three loops and then tying through the center with a further length of ribbon. Fold the napkin to make a little bed for the rose, slip the phial under a fold, and then tie the napkin with the bow.

centerpieces

LEFT Branching stems of pink phalaenopsis orchids have been hand-tied and placed in a tall clear glass cylinder vase filled with pink aluminum wire and suspended orchids. RIGHT This mossed candelabra has been decorated with *Acacia, Stephanandra incisa* 'Crispa,' Portugal laurel, roses, astilbe, hydrangea, and hypericum. Dried bunches of lavender in terra-cotta pots have also been used as extra decoration at its foot.

making a statement

As most celebrations culminate in a large feast, it is inevitable that your table will be the focus, so your centerpieces are of paramount importance—flowers bring luxury, beauty, and fragrance. Floral arrangements can be of differing heights, depending on the size and style of your venue. For any event with more than one hundred guests, you will probably want to include some statement arrangements. For a celebration of over twenty tables, you may want to have taller and more significant arrangements on half of the tables. Statement centerpieces lift the eye around the room, fill the space, and add color. They make the venue look more dressed, which adds gravitas to the event.

creating height

The Victorians, who took entertaining very seriously and who loved to decorate their tables in lavish fashion, used epergnes—huge ornamental centerpieces—or tall lily vases to give their tables presence. Some Victorians even took the exceptional step of having holes carved in their tables so they could incorporate oversized plants such as kentia palms in the decoration of their table.

Modern flower arrangers do not need to take such drastic steps to create an effect, and glass is currently very popular for making a statement with flowers. In recent years, manufacturers have produced an enormous variety of tall shapes to be used for this purpose. Originally, the lily vase was one of the few tall shapes available, but now there are round and square columns, flared vases of all heights and proportions, and huge glass spheres and tanks. The advantage of glass is that it is translucent—you can still see across the table. However, in recent years, there has been a trend to place items inside the vase for added interest and to create a more decorative look. Cellophane creates an icy look and is very effective with petals or fruit. Colored aluminum wire looks great on its own or with suspended waxy flower heads such as anthuriums and orchids. The addition of leaves, grasses, reeds, and twigs to vases creates a more natural feel. By using a vase within a vase, or floral foam rather than water, there are a number of other accessories such as rocks, shells, candy, fruit, and even vegetables that can be used in tall glass vases to add color and interest and make a stunning centerpiece.

LEFT A hand-tied bouquet of cotinus, *Alchemilla mollis*, hydrangea, lilies, trailing amaranthus, and gloriosa has been placed in a tall glass vase filled with gold aluminum wire. This is a substantial arrangement, but the bulk of the display is kept clear of the sight lines of seated guests. RIGHT A metal candelabra has been decorated with ivy, ruscus, and *Viburnum opulus* berries and then filled out with gerberas, *Leucospermum cordifolium*, *Celosia* 'Bombay Fiora,' and 'Peppermint,' 'Milano,' and 'Wow!' roses.

LEFT This candelabra has
been decorated with ruscus,
eucalyptus, and variegated
ivy with *Alchemilla mollis* and
a selection of garden roses
for a predominantly pastel
color theme.
RIGHT A standard topiary tree
for a round wedding table
is made from stephanotis,
camellia, *Brachyglottis*
'Sunshine,' *Viburnum tinus*
berries, hydrangea, 'Talea,'
'Metallina,' and 'Old Dutch'
roses, and green eustoma.

sculptural style Since Tudor times,

height has been achieved by using candelabra. They may be
one of the oldest decorations for a table, and while they
may have lost their essential utilitarian role, they are still
used the most often. They are extremely versatile and can
be dressed up to suit the venue and theme an event.

At my studio, we have many different metal candelabra
that are around 3 ft (1 m) tall and have tall narrow stands
with sturdy bases. The metal can either be spray painted
for a gilded finish or distressed to look like antique rust,
verdigris, or even stone for more rustic events. For an
elaborate feel, the metal can be covered in moss, twigs,
foliage, and even fabric. Moss is one of our most common
coverings, achieved by binding sphagnum or carpet moss
onto the metal. Rosemary, box, or hebe work well for a
foliage covering, and we usually work in exactly the same
way, binding the foliage around the metal so the finished
effect is like topiary. Twigs from the *Betula* and *Salix* trees
are also very effective. In the holiday season we often
spray paint them, and when a "winter wonderland"
theme is required, we often use white-dipped birch
with a glitter finish for added sparkle.

Creating sculptural points of interest in a room
creates ambiance and moves the eye across the venue.
The arrangements also add color, and for evening events, a
greater visual effect can be achieved with pin spotlights.
Many ballrooms already have this feature built into their

lighting systems, but very often outside event-lighting
companies work with the florist to make sure the floral
displays are lit to their best advantage.

Apart from candelabra, other strongly sculptural
forms can be created by making individual topiary
arrangements. Topiaries can take the outline of tree shapes,
such as a pyramid or cone, or the standard shape of a ball
on top of a stem. These are generally constructed using a
trunk made from strong wood such as birch or bamboo,
and a round ball made from moss and chicken wire, or
large spherical blocks of floral foam. Alternatively, "living"
topiaries where flowers are on their natural stems (such as
that on pages 98–99) are also very effective. Favorites
include sunflowers, agapanthus, amaryllis, and nerines,
where the heads are large, but the stems
are thin, long, and elegant.

materials

a glass vase, 3 ft (1 m) tall and
8–10 in (25–20 cm) wide

a length of colored aluminum
floral wire

2 or 3 stems of matching
cymbidium orchids

suspended orchids

This has got to be one of the easiest and most effective ways of making a quick and striking centerpiece.
Cymbidium orchids are available throughout the year and last incredibly well. Although they seem expensive
at first, their longevity as a cut flower makes them one of the most economical flowers.

Step 1 Usually there are about seven
heads on each stem of cymbidium
orchid, so you will need at least two
stems for this design. Remove the
heads from the stem, leaving very
short stalks. Next, cut some lengths
of the aluminum wire and twist it
into curls to place inside the vase.

Step 2 To fill the vase, start with a coil of aluminum wire, placing it at the base of the vase. Next, add some cymbidium heads followed by more coils of aluminum wire and continue alternating flowers and wire until you have filled the entire vase. Fill the vase to the top with water mixed with flower food so all the flower heads have water.

materials

20 yellow calla lilies (*Zantedeschia* 'Florex Gold')

6 sunflowers (*Helianthus* 'Orit')

9 *Celosia* (Cristata Group) 'Bombay Yellow'

6 stems of crab apples (*Malus* 'Cowichan')

4 bunches of *Skimmia confusa* 'Kew Green'

a bunch of *Viburnum tinus* berries

10 stems of *Alchemilla mollis*

6 stems of ornamental kales (*Brassica oleracea* 'White Crane')

20 'Kaliki' mini gerbera

a 12-in (30-cm) straight sided glass bowl

a 16-in (40-cm) floral foam ring

a 3-in (8-cm) pinholder

a roll of floral fix

a roll of floral tie

a few stems of bear grass

sheaf of callas

A low straight-sided glass bowl is one of the most versatile containers you can have. We use them time and time again for arrangements from simple designs using floating candles and flower heads to elaborate rings of flowers. Here, used with a pinholder, you can combine two styles of arrangement to create a striking centerpiece.

Step 1 Soak the floral foam ring and then place the glass bowl inside. Arrange the foliage loosely around the ring, varying the plant material. Place foliage up to the ring but not over the edge of the glass and down to the base covering the plastic base of the ring. Continue until the foam has been completely covered by the greenery. Place some green floral fix onto the bottom of the pinholder and attach it to the center of the glass bowl.

Step 2 Start to add the flowers in groups. This gives the design more impact and makes the color less diluted. Balance the larger-headed flowers around the ring so they do not overpower the smaller flowers.

Step 3 Hand tie the calla lilies so they are spiraled like a sheaf. Bind with wired floral tie and cover the binding with strands of bear grass, also tied. Place the callas on the pinholder to stand upright and add water to the bowl to keep them fresh.

compact arrangements

The low, round, compact arrangement is possibly the most frequently requested shape and style because it can be modified to all budgets and occasions. It is easy to create, adapts to any venue, and can be made to any size. Small versions are produced for side tables and coffee tables. I also prefer to use small round arrangements on a long dining table—I like to zigzag a number of them down the table to leave the center free for large serving dishes. Medium-sized designs are produced as gifts and for the home dining table. Larger arrangements are designed for gracing banqueting dining tables, consoles, or side tables at bigger events. The larger the table, the bigger the floral design needs to be, and very often the type of plant material used will also be correspondingly larger in scale.

LEFT A neat posy of 'Passion' roses and gray *Brachyglottis* 'Sunshine' is very simple and can be repeated as many times as necessary depending on the size of your table. RIGHT For a summer wedding arrangement, this grouping of hydrangea, *Alchemilla mollis*, astrantia, cotinus, blackberry, and garden roses, with individual terra-cotta pots wired into it, gives a charming cottage garden feel.

long tables

Long tables look really well-dressed when you have a floral arrangement about every three or four chairs—every six being the maximum distance before the flowers look too sparse. Often long tables are quite narrow with seating down one side only, and this may dictate small displays or the use of tall thin glass vases or candelabra. On a good-sized banqueting table, which is usually about 5 ft (1.5 m) wide, a compact arrangement about 14 in (35 cm) in diameter will be around the right scale. Alternatively, you can use fewer linear arrangements, which will fill the space better.

As a general rule, when creating a mixed flower arrangement, I usually choose five different types of flowers and use three different types of foliage. In the winter months, ivy berries are a staple foliage for covering the foam, mixed with members of the viburnum family, with *Viburnum tinus* being the most popular. In the summer, herbs provide great fillers, along with lovely textural foliages such as the silver *Brachyglottis* 'Sunshine' or the fluffy lime green *Alchemilla mollis*. The perfect height for a low arrangement is just above the top of the wine glasses, and we are often asked to add petals and votives around the edge of the arrangements for summer weddings. For long tables it is lovely to connect the scattered petals and votives to link the arrangements and draw the eye down the table.

OPPOSITE A glass bowl is lined with leaves and floral foam and filled with ivy berries; hydrangea; double pink eustoma; 'Talea' and 'Sweet Akito,' and 'Espérance' roses. BELOW Late summer roses, green hydrangea, green zinnia, some orange-tinged early *Viburnum opulus* berries, and fluffy sprigs of cotinus fill a verdigris-covered urn.

round tables

The height of the flowers and foliage of compact arrangements is usually less than 14 in (35 cm) off the table surface, including the container. They might incorporate candles, which rise higher from the mass of the arrangement. If the bulk of the arrangement is much larger than 16 in (40 cm) it starts to obscure the view across the table and hinders enjoyment. Most banqueting tables are 5–6 ft (1.5–2 m) round tables, and guests are rarely able to talk to each other across the table because of ambient noise. However, it is always desirable to keep low arrangements just tall enough to have great impact and to be seen above the glassware, but not so tall as to obscure the guests' view across the table.

The current vogue is for compact textural arrangements. Most often these are round, but geometric containers—such as my favorite, the cube vase—gives them a slightly more contemporary look. Elongated oval or rectangular versions work well on long tables. A signature of my compact flower arrangements is to customize the base of the arrangement so that the arrangement has a more sculptural feel. This can make a cheap plastic container look special. It has the added bonus of being inexpensive enough for you to give away to your guests when the event is over. Rhododendron, laurel, and aspidistra leaves are among the least expensive options for this type of wrapping. Other favorites are heather, rosemary, and lavender, which are more expensive, both because they use more material and labor and because the materials themselves are initially more costly.

compact arrangements **103**

ABOVE Floral foam balls have been massed with the daisy-like heads of the green-centered chrysanthemum 'Dark Rosy Reagan.'

BELOW A dome of 'Avalanche' roses have been arranged in a glass cylinder filled with slices of kiwi fruit for a fresh summer centerpiece.

OPPOSITE A green-leafed bowl filled with a rounded display of *Viburnum opulus*, hydrangea, blackberries, and 'Grand Prix,' 'Milano,' and 'Milva' roses.

dense shapes

Massed arrangements are created from one type of flower. The use of one variety en masse is very arresting and effective; some of the most memorable parties I have designed have used massed flowers on every table. The impact from the concentration of color and texture is immediate. Individual flowers are not seen, only the shape they form. Good floral design should stand the test of time and appear effortless and natural, and massed flowers achieve this every time.

New floral fads come and go, but simple blocks of color always look good on a table and work as well in a historic interior as they do in a minimalist apartment. By far the most common flower to use this way is the rose. Roses are available in so many shades, sizes, and qualities they make the perfect flower for any occasion. For the amateur flower arranger, using one type of flower can make it easier to budget and purchase flowers. For events with lower budgets, inexpensive flowers such as carnations or chrysanthemums can be used to great effect.

Get the compact effect using a tightly packed hand-tied arrangement, especially with lower-budget arrangements or occasional table arrangements. If the plant material is really soft or needs to last a long time, we use crumpled chicken wire in a bowl of water, especially if the weather is humid or hot. But often for events, plant material only has to last a few hours, so longevity is immaterial.

materials

6 red *Rosa* 'Grand Prix'

6 dark pink *Rosa* 'Milano'''

6 yellow *Rosa* 'Ilios!'

6 burgundy *Rosa* 'Black Baccara'

3 peach *Rosa* 'Cherry Brandy'

3 pink *Rosa* 'Beauty by Oger'

4–5 bunches of dried lavender

a small floral foam rackette

a pair of scissors

a bundle of heavy wire

a length of ribbon

long lavender arrangement

This simple design is very versatile and can be made with fresh or dried flowers. Here, we have used a combination of dried lavender with fresh roses. Instead of lavender you could use rosemary, box, or wheat and a mass of roses of one color or alternate stripes rather than the rainbow effect here.

Step 1 Soak the foam in water. Split the lavender into small bunches with all the flower heads the same height. Trim them so the flowers are about ¾ in (2 cm) above the edge of the foam. Bend the wires and use them to pin each bunch of the lavender to the foam. Try to place the pin for each bunch at the same level so that the pinning looks neat. Continue until the foam is completely concealed.

Step 2 When all the lavender is secured, you are ready to add the flowers. You could use lots of different types of flowers for this design, but flat-headed flowers work best. Gerbera, sunflowers, and ranunculus all work well, but roses are my favorite. Cut the rose head off the stem leaving around 1½ in (4 cm) and carefully push the rose head into the soaked foam. Tie with the ribbon and make a bow to finish the design.

materials

100 stems of bright pink zinnias

bright pink aggregate rocks

3 low dishes

3 small plastic glasses

9 bright pink faux butterflies

a pair of sharp scissors

a roll of floral bind wire

pretty pink line-up

Monochromatic displays are simple to construct and can be very effective. I love the hot colors of zinnias and have used them here with some coordinating sand. Brightly colored aggregate rocks used to be found only in tropical fish stores, but now they are a staple in the florist supply stores. They are an inexpensive way of making a bright container for flowers or potted plants.

Step 1 Strip all the lower foliage from the stems of the zinnias and begin to make a small posy by spiraling the stems. Repeat three times, holding them very carefully because their stems are quite fragile. Secure with floral bind wire.

Step 2 Carefully cut the plastic glasses down at the rim so they are flush with the top of the glass bowls. Place the glasses in the center of the bowls and add pink rocks around them until they are flush with the edge of the container. Fill with water mixed with flower food then add each bunch to the center of one of the containers. Attach the wired butterflies to the tops and sides of the posies.

OPPOSITE The trough on the left includes a slightly different summer combination of flowers, giving a more peachy pink effect by using pink *Astilbe* x *arendsii* 'Amerika,' lime *Alchemilla mollis*, and 'Pinky Flair' hypericum contrasted with the dark purple *Cotinus coggygria* 'Royal Purple.'

simple, long, and low

Thin narrow glass troughs are perfect for creating neat designs for long tables. This gorgeous summer arrangement looks stunning on a dining table and gives the added bonus of providing little gifts for your guests to take away at the end of a leisurely summer lunch. To create some structure with a vase like this, you can tape a grid across the top using ordinary tape.

materials

15 *Rosa* 'Versilla'

10 dark red 'Viking' dahlias

10 calla lilies (*Zantedeschia* 'Chopin')

10 *Asclepias* 'Alessa'

10 stems of *Ajania pacifica* 'Silver and Gold'

3 bunches of *Panicum virgatum* 'Squaw'

10 stems of *Achillea* 'Moonshine'

10 stems of *Astrantia major* 'Claret'

5 stems of *Eryngium* 'Orion Questar'

5 bunches of *Galax urceolata* leaves

10 stems of *Nectaroscordum siculum*

a long glass trough

a roll of floral bind wire

Step 1 To make little posies, it is very important to cut down the flowers and foliage and clean any foliage from below the head of the stem. When all the plant material has been stripped, lay out the flowers in neat piles of the same variety. As this is going to be a very small posy, you will need to hold the plant material at the top of the stem near the head. Take a strong central flower such as a rose and then place more plant material to the left of the first flower until you have created a small fan of plant material. At this stage, you need to twist the flowers, taking them into your other hand. Then add a further five stems. Keep spiraling and twisting them until you have about fifteen stems in each bunch, including three roses.

Step 2 Add the galax leaves to the edge to create a collar. It is essential that the stems are clean so when you tie at the binding point, the lower area is free from debris and the water will not get contaminated. Tie firmly with floral bind wire. Continue making four more bunches in the same way.

Step 3 Recut the stems and place the posies into the trough using the galax collar to keep them in place. Fill the trough with water and flower food.

candles

Adding candlelight to a table creates an ambiance and gives any event a really great atmosphere. Candlelight is magical and sensuous, and certainly all my earliest memories of candlelight are associated with happy times, with ritual and celebration: the blowing out of candles on a birthday cake; the glowing candlelight at Christmas with all the expectation of the festive season; hurricane lamps around a warm bay while eating al fresco at the end of a perfect summer's day; candles burning in bottles in trattoria, where the wax takes on a new sculptural form that is so invitingly tactile. Candlelight is deeply romantic and evocative and is one of the first things we all think of when we wish to make an inviting and warm table to entertain friends.

LEFT A long, low centerpiece in which *Alchemilla mollis*, green hydrangea, ivy foliage trails, hypericum, and sunflowers surround a yellow pillar candle.

RIGHT On a long banqueting table set for a wedding, low glass bowls alternate with tall crystal candelabra—the change in pace brings dynamism to the whole table setting. Both the rings around the candelabra and the bowls are filled with ivy berries, hydrangea, double pink lisianthus, 'Talea,' 'Sweet Akito,' and 'Espérance' roses.

LEFT It is a nice idea to place decorations at table level to complement the height of a candelabra. This metal one has been covered with flowering *Prunus* and sprigs of gypsophila to echo the pink candles. A ring of ivy berries, 'Sweet Akito' roses, pale pink ranunculus and gypsophila encircling the base offer visual balance.

OPPOSITE Glass votives are filled with gypsophila, ranunculus, muscari, and sprigs of lilac, and placed on an ornate wirework candelabra. A garland for the table was created by wiring bunches of flowers to asparagus fern.

candelabra

Candles can be used to dress up an event or in a very casual and informal role. When I want to make a venue look very grand and formal, I use tall table candelabra. For more casual events, the candles are often worked into the flower display itself. For a more contemporary look, we rely on glass votives that are now available in a tantalizing array of colors, shapes, and sizes.

To get the best from your candles, it is important to remember that they perform best when they have been stored in a really cold place, or even in a refrigerator for a few hours before they are lit. The cold temperature makes them burn more evenly and slowly, which helps to build up a good pool of wax that in turn allows the flame to keep going. To prevent uneven burning or erratic flames, avoid placing them in drafts or air-conditioned rooms.

In our arrangements, we always wire and tape our candles in place by creating legs. Usually this is done with heavy floral stub wires, but if you do not have access to these, you can use wooden skewers or bamboo stakes to the same effect. If you do not have floral tape, you can use ordinary tape or electrical tape, sold in hardware stores, to anchor the sticks to the candles. Failing all of the above, if you have a pillar candle, you can anchor it in the foam by pressing the base of the candle in the foam and then placing sturdy sticks vertically in the foam to secure the candle. In candelabra I generally like to secure my candle with foam fix or reusable putty so they are stuck firmly into the candleholder—you don't want them to topple! If the candlesticks are glass and you need to camouflage the mechanism, a layer of plastic wrap or cellophane around the base helps keep them snug in the candleholder.

Whatever the shape and size of the candle, the one thing that unites them all is the wick. This is generally made from braided cotton and should be trimmed to about ½ in (1 cm) and should never be longer than 1 in (2.5 cm), as it will smoke. Never trim the wick too short, which can cause the wick to drip. Never leave a lit candle unattended.

Some venues do not allow the use of candles, either because they are too dirty or too dangerous, or because they cause problems with smoke alarms. Some historic homes do not allow them because it increases their insurance premium, so always seek permission from the venue owner before you decide to incorporate them into your designs. If you are desperate to use candles but your chosen venue prohibits their use, you can now find very good imitation candles and votives on the market. They are effective, and some are very authentic-looking.

materials

10 stems of flowering *Forsythia* x *intermedia* 'Spectabilis'

a bunch of ivy berries (*Hedera helix*)

a bunch of trailing ivy (*Hedera helix*)

a bunch of mimosa (*Acacia dealbata*)

a bunch of yellow tulips (*Tulipa* 'Fancy Frill')

3 pots of yellow *Ranunculus* 'Pauline Gold'

a bunch of *Helleborus foetidus*

a bunch of 'Yellow Queen' hyacinths

a bunch of *Narcissus* 'Dick Wilden'

a metal candelabra covered in birch (*Betula pendula*)

3 blocks of floral foam

a low square tray

a spool of reel wire

a water bottle

a bamboo stake

a few heavy stub wires

blooming spring candelabra

Candelabra are a perennial favorite, and I love making them into living topiary shapes by adding greenery or flowers for special events. Rosemary, ivy, and box are some of my favorite foliages to use at any time of the year, but in the spring, blossom or flowering stems of all types look great wound around the structure, and later in the year twigs and berries can give the same arrangement an autumnal feel.

Step 1 Take a tall metal candelabra with a heavy base. Make sure your forsythia has been conditioned well before adding it to the candelabra as that will help it to last better. Add some lengths of blossom starting from the bottom and working each branch along the lengths of the arms of the candelabra, binding with reel wire.

Step 2 Place the candelabra in the tray and add some cut blocks of soaked floral foam to the top and tape in place. Make sure the ends of the blossom are stuck into the foam so they will be able to benefit from the moisture in the foam. Take a water bottle and mist the forsythia to keep it fresh.

Step 3 Add the foliage to the base, working down in height from the center to the edge to create a natural effect, as if the flowers were growing around the base of a tree. Cut a bamboo stake in three and place in hole in the bottom of each of the pots of ranunculus so you can anchor them in the floral foam around the candelabra.

4

Step 4 Add the flowers to the base, placing them as naturalistically as possible so the flowers look like they are growing. You may need to use some internal heavy wires through the center of the stems of narcissus, ranunculus, and hyacinths to help strengthen them. Add as much water as you can to the base when the candelabra has been positioned and mist well with water to keep fresh.

LEFT A ring of foam surrounds three cylinder vases with floating candles. Groups of colored shells have been matched to celosia and multi-colored roses to create a very textural arrangement.

RIGHT Two rings of floral foam have been placed on shallow wicker trays and then placed on top of each other. Into the center a hurricane lamp has been placed and a thick pillar candle inserted. To cover the foam there is a late summer combination of *Alchemilla mollis*, *Weigela* 'Sparkling Fantasy,' 'Black Baccara,' 'Mama Mia' roses, red dahlias, 'Royal Fantasy' lilies, and *Gaillardia* 'Kobold.'

smaller candles

Despite the fact that I work with flowers practically every day and have access to some of the most beautiful blooms available, I am often short of time to arrange my own flowers! Both my favorite shortcuts for decorating my own table at home rely heavily on the use of candles. The first is to use large deep glass bowls filled with floating flower heads and candles. The second is to decorate the table with simple trails of ivy and dot votives and small pots of simply arranged flowers throughout the trails. In fact, this can look very effective without flowers if you mix pillar candles and votives among the trails. Another very casual and simple trick is to use lots of mirror disks and place votives on top of them to reflect flickering candlelight.

A mass of votives is very welcoming, and when the budget is limited, we often recommend a table full of little lights for hallways. Another inexpensive tip is to use glass hurricane lamps and fill the base with petals—if you use garden roses, you get the sweet warm aroma of the flowers as you pass. The petals also protect the glass from the wax, so they are practical as well as pretty. We often anchor candles in hurricane lamps with sand or colored aquarium gravel. This again can add color, but also helps protect the glass and saves time as the wax gets trapped in the sand and does not take so much time to clean off!

Everyone loves fragrance, and there are masses of gorgeous scented candles around in a myriad of designs. While I often use scented candles for occasional tables and for cocktail parties, I rarely use them on tables where a full meal will be served. The scent of the candle can often overpower the flavors and aromas of the food.

Candles easily get dirty, and if you have large candles that you wish to use again, you will find that they attract dirt and dust. The best way to clean them is to use some rough and inexpensive panty hose. The finer the hosiery, the less effective they are at cleaning, since they are not so gently abrasive as cheap hosiery. Olive oil and a soft cloth are also an option for the more fastidious of us!

materials

a bunch of ivy berries (*Hedera helix*)

a bunch of *Skimmia japonica* 'Rubella'

7 *Rosa* 'Grand Prix'

5 stems of *Hypericum* 'Excellent Flair'

8 small waxed pears

a stem of gold and burgundy cymbidium orchid

a burgundy pillar candle

2 blocks of floral foam

a selection of heavy stub wires

a roll of floral tape

a glass vase

dinner centerpiece

This simple design is very adaptable and can be used for any season and with pretty much any flower or greenery combination. In the fall and winter I love to include fruits and seed heads in my arrangement for texture and color. At Christmastime we arrange lots of these, using only a selection of winter foliage, berries, cones, and a few cinnamon sticks.

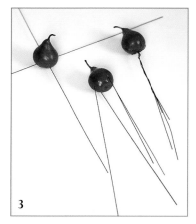

Step 1 After soaking the floral foam, place one and a half blocks vertically in the container. It is important that the foam is above the edge of the container so you can create a rounded shape. Secure it with tape. Cut a bamboo stake into four or make hairpins with the heavy wires to tape to the bottom of the candle to anchor it in the foam.

Step 2 Starting with the ivy berries, place small sprigs around the foam at different heights and depths. Add the skimmia and the hypericum berries, spreading them evenly until most of the green floral foam has been obscured.

Step 3 Take one wire and pass it through the bottom of a waxed pear, then pass another wire through at right angles to the first. At this stage the wires resemble a cross. Bend them all down together at the bottom of the pear and twist so the four wire legs become one. Trim the wires to 1½ in (3.5 cm). If you cannot get waxed pears, use natural ones or spray paint them for more color.

Step 4 It is best to place the flowers first, then add fruit in any gaps you may have. First, take the orchid and cut it into three pieces. Place into the foam, then add the roses at different heights and depths around the vase. Finally, anchor the wires of the pears firmly in the foam.

materials

a 16-in (40-cm) floral foam ring in a tray

8 candles

8 candleholders

10 stems of *Eupatorium purpureum*

15 stems of *Eustoma grandiflorum* 'Mariachi Blue'

9 stems each of 'Beauty By Oger,' 'Cool Water,' and 'Pacific Blue' roses

20 stems of blue scabious

20 stems of *Zinnia elegans*

7 stems of *Cotinus coggygria* 'Royal Purple'

grouped floral ring

Floral foam rings are very useful for creating designs that incorporate candles. Rings range from around 4 in (10 cm) in diameter to 30 in (75 cm) or more, so there is a perfect size for any round table. Grouping flowers together is also an easy way to use a more diverse color and texture range.

Step 1 Soak the foam for a few minutes in water mixed with flower food. When the air bubbles cease to rise, the foam is ready for action. Plastic candleholders can be found in two different sizes and help to anchor the candles in the foam. If you are unable to source the candleholders, you can just use bamboo stakes or wires and floral tape to secure them to the candles.

Step 2 Add the foliage and flowers in groups working from the inside out, making sure the plastic rim below the foam is hidden. Move the ring around as you work on it so you are adding the flowers evenly. Take care to balance the color and texture as you work around the ring.

Step 3 Continue with the groups, adding the softer stems carefully by keeping your hand close to the foam and gently easing in the stems. Zinnias are particularly fragile and should only be displayed in foam for event work when longevity is not the main issue. Finally, mist everything with water.

special events

BELOW AND OPPOSITE When you are thinking about the kind of flowers you want for your wedding, put some ideas together to act as a starting point for discussion with your florist. These are the swatches and menu cards my colleague Sarah collected for her wedding, together with some sprigs of stephanotis and ivy berries, some of her chosen flowers.

weddings

For most couples, the wedding reception is the party of a lifetime—it celebrates their marriage and marks the culmination of many months of planning. The happy couple want the event to be memorable and to bring together their loved ones and two sets of friends and family. When it comes to the floral decorations, the possibilities are endless and, whatever the budget you are working with, it is possible to create a memorable and imaginative reception. Very often choosing the flowers involves a number of meetings with all of your main suppliers, and the florist is no exception.

planning the big day
Usually if you are interviewing a florist you have chosen to work with, you may have an early meeting to outline a quotation and ascertain a realistic budget that you are happy with. This can be a give-and-take situation: you can suggest a budget and your florist can give you an idea of what they can achieve for you. Often, if you are on a limited budget, this is the best way of approaching the wedding decorations. Or, as is normally the case, you give a "wish list" of every single place you would like to see flowers and a quotation is prepared, which usually exceeds the budget; then a further meeting is arranged to cut the decorations to suit a newly agreed budget. For most people, flowers are one of those commodities they would love to have everywhere, but realistically there are some areas that are more important and should command most of the budget. After the bridal bouquets, making the tables beautiful is certainly a priority. If there is money left over, think about where to have some tall statement flowers that everyone will see. Very often the first visit to a florist may involve looking at a scrapbook of ideas incorporating one's favorite flowers, colors, and so on, and also the start of the wedding scheme, with swatches of materials, sketches of the dress, and the style of the invitations. This is the start of a "mood board" for the wedding.

LEFT A group of vases all holding a single variety of flowers makes a statement at the entrance to a wedding. White gladioli, white amaryllis, gardenia heads, cymbidium orchids, and hydrangea heads are all on display in appropriately chosen glass vases.

BELOW A collection of quirkily shaped vases with just a few stems makes a unique occasional table. A single head of hydrangea, a stem of lysimachia, and three stems of scented tuberose emerge from colored glass vases.

ABOVE RIGHT Mushroom baskets filled with autumnal hydrangea and 'Margaret Merril' and 'Old Dutch' roses are used to line the entrance.

OPPOSITE This imposing arrangement set on a pedestal is of autumnal foliages with white amaryllis, *Euphorbia fulgens*, green hydrangea, and green cymbidium orchids with a touch of red cotoneaster berries and some hanging trails of red amaranthus.

styling the wedding

When my colleague Sarah was planning her wedding, she had a very clear idea about what kinds of colors she wanted for the flowers and how that would fit with her autumnal theme. Having chosen an elegant heritage home in a beautiful wooded National Trust park as the venue, she set the wedding date for a time when the park would be in all its autumnal glory. To make more detailed plans for the wedding flowers, we fixed a date for a site visit to "walk the course" and look at the venue and all the rooms we would be using for the celebration. From this, one has to take note of the interior decoration and pay consideration to the rules and regulations of the particular venue. In Sarah's case, the venue's ban on naked flames meant that we would have to work a scheme around this. We decided to use battery-operated votives and candles (which are now amazingly realistic, coated in real wax and smelling waxy!) and use topiary trees to get height in our dining room arrangements and continue the fall theme.

Sarah was using a lot of rooms and needed decorations for five or six large rooms plus some communal areas. We decided on large arrangements for the ceremony, some garlands on the stairs, and some huge mantelpiece

RIGHT A posy of hydrangea and garden roses is tied to the back of the bride and bridegroom's chairs with ivory ribbon.

BELOW Four huge urns of flowers flank the corners of the dining room. Topiary trees are used for half the tables for this wedding to add height to the room. We usually get height by using candelabra or tall glass vases, but for this venue, candles were not allowed. The tables were named after the bride's favorite flowers.

OPPOSITE Low arrangements for the tables were made out of baskets covered in lichen twigs and moss and filled with hydrangea, ivy berries, *Brachyglottis* 'Sunshine,' and 'Metallina,' 'Vendella,' 'Talea,' and 'Old Dutch' roses. Woven throughout the design are trails of scented stephanotis.

ABOVE Pedestal with autumnal foliage and white amaryllis, white *Euphorbia fulgens*, white 'Helvetia' lilies, cymbidium orchids, green hydrangea, and moluccella.

arrangements for the other rooms, which could be seen while people were standing and chatting and enjoying drinks. For the occasional tables, a selection of three vases, each filled with one type of flower en masse gave a modern yet classic look to the flowers.

Sarah had already chosen a café-au-lait color for her bridesmaids' dresses and had used a brown sepia effect for her invitations and menu cards. There are a few roses which capture this color, but they are rare and so we had to make sure that we could find them overseas; we imported 'Metallina' from Ecuador and 'Julia's Baby' from an English rose supplier who grows in Kenya when the English climate is no longer able to produce roses. Sarah was also eager to have lots of scent, so stephanotis plants and stems of beautiful cream tuberose flowers were ordered, as well as lots of heads of gardenias from growers in Denmark. When the finished designs, with their varied sources, were all in place, one could not help but think about the magic of the multicultural industry that, as floral designers, we just take for granted!

materials

a bunch of peach
Ranunculus Clooney

a bunch of cream
Ranunculus Clooney

10 stems of *Viburnum opulus*

2 bunches of *Skimmia japonica*

a bunch of ivy berries
(*Hedera helix*)

9 *Rosa* 'Grand Prix'

an 8-in (20-cm) foam ball

a block of floral foam

a sturdy silver birch branch

a bag of quick-drying cement

a sturdy terra-cotta pot

2 medium-length screws

a water bottle

floral tree

Nature is a great teacher, and any shape found in the wild is a great inspiration for a floral design. The classic standard round topiary shape never really goes out of style and makes a great design that is versatile enough to be used at formal or informal events.

Step 1 Cut the branch to the desired length—usually somewhere around 3 ft (1 m) will give you enough clearance to be able to see across the table under the flower ball. Mix some quick-drying cement and anchor the branch in the center of the terra-cotta pot. Let it dry overnight so it is firmly set. When the cement is hard, place two screws in the top of the birch poles. Soak the foam brick and ball until the air bubbles cease to rise. Place the soaked floral foam ball on top of the pole anchored by the two screws. Cut the floral foam block to cover the cement at the base.

Step 2 Using the greenery, establish the shape of the topiary. Make sure you keep twisting the tree so you are working on all sides, and move away from the design frequently to check that you are creating a good shape. When you have completed the ball, add some foliage to the top of the base.

Step 3 Add the flowers, taking each variety in turn and making sure to add types and colors evenly around the design. Add the softer lime green viburnum last so you can place them in any dark spots. Keep your hand close to the foam to allow you to sink their soft stems into it without damage. Keep well misted.

RIGHT A classic autumnal wedding topiary using skimmia and ivy berries as the base with 'Vendella,' 'Illusion,' and 'Old Dutch' roses with hydrangea. Trails of scented stephanotis are used to soften the shape.

LEFT Sorbus, forsythia, ivy, and moluccella are the foliage base for this blue and white summer arrangement, which includes blue hydrangea, delphinium, and echinops with white 'Casa Blanca' lilies, agapanthus, hydrangea, and 'Iceberg' roses.

LEFT This tiny brass altar vase was filled with 'Blue Globe' echinops, eryngium, *Alchemilla mollis*, and 'Vendella,' 'Peppermint,' and garden roses.

RIGHT The font has been decorated with a ring of matching summer flowers set around a hurricane lamp and pillar candle. Bachelor's buttons, hydrangea, and scabious have been mixed with echinops and eryngium with groups of white hydrangea and roses.

BELOW RIGHT The pew end decorations are made from garden roses with *Alchemilla mollis*, cornflower, lavender, and eryngium.

church flowers

Weddings that take place in a church or other place of worship usually require a number of large arrangements, particularly up close to the altar to flank the ceremony. These are usually placed on pedestals or plinths, and most churches have a stock of them for you to use. However, there are always one or two other spots that are crying out for a few flowers. Each church will have its own views on how the flowers should be displayed on the altar, and it is always best to ask permission to decorate. Some churches have some fine altar vases, which you will possibly be able to use. Very often we create a long trailing arrangement for the altar, and move it to the long bride's table at the reception. There are usually one or two other tables worth decorating, such as one positioned near the exit to the church and perhaps one in the vestibule to greet the guests as they arrive. I am also a fan of pew ends, as the central aisle is the focus of attention for the wedding, so if the pews are suitable, I usually suggest at least five along each side and more if the aisle is long.

For this church wedding, the table decorations were designed with the bridal party flowers in mind, and this dictated the composition of the flowers in the church. The fabric for the bridesmaids' dresses and an illustration by the mother of the bride, which became the invitation and the menu card, were our starting point for the flower selection. The bride made her final selection of flowers just a few weeks before the wedding, when she was able to come to my studio and see the full selection of colors available in tones of blue. As a receding color, blue is not always the best color for a church, where the light can often be dim and you want to make an impression. However, the wedding took place in a small village church that is light and where the decoration is simple, so the blue and white theme worked well. Loose country early summer foliage and flowers were used to create a casual country feel.

LEFT Hundreds of individual flower heads of the white daisy *Chrysanthemum* 'White Reagan' have been massed on floral foam balls with a central candle. The bottom of the floral foam is sliced off before construction so the balls sit securely without rolling.
RIGHT The massed balls have been interspersed between silver candelabra adorned with daisy garlands that also snake along the table. A single flower sits on each napkin.

outdoor receptions
For weddings white and green continue to be the most popular shades by far, and even though I am a fan of color, I have to admit there is something rather special about an all-white wedding. Simplicity is also very arresting, and one of my favorite ways to work with white is to use one type of flower. White orchids, roses, peonies, lily-of-the-valley, and sweet peas all work well en masse, but one of my favorites is the humble daisy. Everyone old or young loves the daisy, and just a few stems in a vase will cause more comment from guests than the fanciest arrangement of exotic florists' blooms. I particularly like the wild ox-eye daisies that grow in profusion by many roadsides—they are the national flower of Latvia. Of the daisies cultivated for cut-flower production, my preferred variety is the margarita daisy, which is grown mostly in Italy. They are lovely massed together, but they also look fabulous as a plant on a table or as huge standard varieties to line a celebration along an aisle or pathway.

For the simple yet striking flower display shown on these pages, however, I chose to use spray chrysanthemum daisies. Often given very bad press, the spray chrysanthemum has fallen a long way down the flower charts from the days when it was considered the highest of flowers by the Chinese. Once the flower was depicted on the Japanese imperial flag, and although the Japanese still hold a national festival devoted to the flower on September 9 each year, widespread production has rendered the flower common and therefore less desirable. However, I love to use the large standard blooms and heads of the spray varieties en masse, as here on balls or in domes or wired together as daisy chains. One of the huge strengths of the chrysanthemum flower is that it is strong and lasts well—often up to three weeks in water—so it holds up well as a chain and in these oasis balls it should easily last two weeks. There are also many shades of chrysanthemum to suit different themes, many of which are part of the *Chrysanthemum* Reagan Series, whose colors range from yellow 'Sunny Reagan' to deep 'Ruby Red Reagan.'

formal receptions

The practice of adorning tables with foliage, herbs, flowers, and petals has been an integral part of weddings as far back as ancient Greece and Rome and has endured to this day. Whatever the budget, the table flowers are often the most significant design of the wedding flowers after the bride's wedding bouquet. The range of table decoration, from tiny decorations for occasional tables at cocktail receptions to huge grand centerpieces for lavish ballrooms, varies enormously. If you are being formally seated, the main consideration is whether your guests will be accommodated on round or long tables. Round tables come in many sizes, but for wedding banqueting the most common size is a 5- or 6-ft (1.5- or 2-m) diameter round table. This makes comfortable seating for eight people and up to twelve for the larger tables.

It is very common to have two or more designs on round tables, some of them tall to fill the space and some low for interest. Usually the high designs are achieved by using candelabra with thin stems or narrow glass vases so the view across the table is not unduly obscured. Long tables vary in width and start from 30 in (75 cm), which are more commonly used when space is tight. These thinner tables make table decoration a challenge—if you have guests facing each other down both sides and a number of wine and water glasses, it does not leave much room for the flowers once the table is set and all the china, flatware, and glassware is in place. These long tables are best suited to candelabra or tall glass vases as well. If that is out of your budget, dotting a number of small containers down each table is one option, or even less expensive is using small potted plants.

OPPOSITE The candelabra set on some of the round banqueting tables have been decorated with ruscus, eucalyptus, and variegated ivy with garden roses.

OPPOSITE BELOW Garden roses, hydrangea, and *Brachyglottis* 'Sunshine' have been tied together as chairbacks to decorate the top table.

RIGHT Any floral decorations set around the room on occasional tables need to be large in scale to make an impact. These giant candelabra have been decorated with the same combination of flowers and foliage as their smaller counterparts set on the dining tables, with the addition of white delphinium, peonies, and stephanotis trails around the arching base.

BELOW A tall pedestal of pink and green hydrangeas, cream and pink delphinium, and long-stemmed roses with scented lilies makes a statement for the ceremony. RIGHT This beautiful verdigris urn is filled with the same combination of flowers and foliage and is placed on the bar to carry the theme.

OPPOSITE One statement piece is better than lots of little arrangements as it gets noticed far more. If the budget is limited, it is always better to spend it on having one grand arrangement that matches the theme and provides a focus for the guests. This huge silver vase has been filled with giant dahlias, lilies, 'Milano' and 'Aqua' roses, scented tuberose, and gladioli.

large-scale displays
When planning a wedding, it is important to give some overall thought to the whole space, so very often we recommend that, as well as using some tall arrangements on the dining tables, you include one or two large statement pieces. There are always lots of other tables and areas that can be enhanced by an accent arrangement or a large centerpiece. It is always better to have one or two grand displays than a number of smaller ones, which may be missed by most of the guests. These often take the form of urns on plinths or, if you are using a venue such as an historic house, there are often features such as mantelpieces or console tables that are perfect for long, drooping arrangements. These will sit above eye level so everyone can see them even if they are standing at a cocktail reception, and it makes more use of the flowers.

Other key spots to decorate are the bride's table or seating plan, the bars, the cake table and the cake itself, or around the outer edges of the venue. It is lovely to have a gorgeous bowl of coordinating flowers on the bride's table when the guests arrive, at the welcome area, or on the bar where the guests will receive their first drink.

Large arrangements like the ones shown on this spread require a lot of foliage to make a statement, as well as long-stemmed and large-headed flowers. We generally specify taller flowers such as delphinium, gladioli, and eremurus and varieties with large heads such as oriental lilies, hydrangea, peonies, textural celosia, or giant dahlias. At least a third all these arrangements are foliage, so it is very important to have some tall foliage, such as forsythia, rhododendron, and sorbus, as well as some lovely trailing greenery, such as long ruscus and ivies, at the edge of the arrangements to soften the look.

materials

2 bunches of fountain grass (*Panicum virgatum* 'Fountain')

2 bunches of pale pink *Astilbe* 'Europa'

a bunch of dark pink *Astilbe* 'Cattleya'

3 bunches of *Skimmia* x *confusa* 'Kew Green'

2 bunches of ivy berries (*Hedera helix*)

10 stems of *Dahlia* 'Boy Scout'

10 stems of *Rosa* 'Illusion'

20 stems of *Rosa* 'Cool Water'

10 stems of *Rosa* 'Nicole'

10 stems of *Eustoma* 'Kyoto Silver Blue'

7 stems of *Hydrangea* 'Green Shadow'

a silver-leaf boat-style container

a length of 2-in (5-cm) chicken wire

side table arrangement

Long low vases are making a comeback as they allow you to design a horizontal arrangement that looks great on console tables, pianos, or particularly small tables at wedding receptions. We chose chicken wire to make this design since there is a lot of soft plant material that benefits from being in water rather than foam.

Step 1 Cut a piece of 2-in (5-cm) chicken wire about the length of the container. Crumple the mesh and fit it snugly in the container. Make sure it rises above the container as shown. It should be snug enough so you can pick up the empty container by the wire without it falling out.

Step 2 Fill with water mixed with flower food and begin to add your foliage to establish a good outline for the arrangement. I usually start with the stronger woody foliages such as ivy berries and skimmia and use the more delicate grasses at the end. Make sure the different varieties of foliage are at varying heights and depths to create a strong outline to the design.

Step 3 Add the larger-headed flowers, then the stronger-stemmed varieties, leaving the weaker astilbe and eustoma to last. The chicken wire aided by the foliage will give you a good structure in which to place the flowers. It is important to vary the angle and the depth of the flowers so you achieve a lovely, full, rounded look to the design from all sides.

BELOW Dyed blue roses were massed with blue hydrangea, white hydrangea, and white roses for a birthday dinner featuring team colors for a Chelsea soccer fanatic.

RIGHT A stationery box is filled with colored roses to match the stripes: 'Milano,' 'Mama Mia,' 'Black Baccara,' 'Cool Water,' 'Barbie,' and the white 'Bianca' dyed blue.

birthdays

The celebration of birthdays is thought to have originated in Persia and began with the cult of Mithras. The marking of birthdays today is fairly universal, offering an annual opportunity for a party or gathering of some sort. Most cultures also have a coming-of-age party, usually at eighteen or twenty-one, which normally accompanies a larger celebration, and many of these occasions involve flowers. Certain key ages after that stand out, such as the attaining of each decade—we are often asked to provide the flowers for fortieth birthday parties, for example. Table decorations vary in each culture according to tradition and budget, but flowers are a central part of the theme.

LEFT For a children's summer birthday party, mixed posies of *Alchemilla mollis,* 'Beauty by Oger,' 'Amalia,' and yellow dot spray roses, and achillea have been placed in glasses decorated inside with layers of matching sand.
RIGHT A small arrangement in a tiny Styrofoam cup in the same color combination is placed on the birthday cake.
BELOW RIGHT Single stems of miniature sunflowers stand in small terra-cotta pots.

kalanchoe or tiny African violets, pansies, or violas. If I do choose flowers, I will use simple inexpensive ones cut short in petite containers. Recycled yogurt jars are one of my favorite containers filled with seasonal flowers. Single flowers arranged in pots as if they are growing is also a great inexpensive way to decorate a table. Choose simple daisy-shaped flowers like Germini or mini sunflowers.

Favorite sports or hobbies often provide inspiration for birthday parties for men, whether it is mossed sculptural horse heads for the racing fan or sand and seashell arrangements for the boat lover. By far the most common choice is to use the colors of a favored sports team. This often means lots of bright combinations that include white as well. Rather than mix a color with white, I prefer to use them separately in individual containers—I am not particularly keen on mixing strong primary colors with white as it looks quite harsh unless you add lots of green foliage or some secondary colors. Other suitable choices for men's birthday parties are to use herbs, particularly some of the lovely growing topiaries such as standard lavenders or rosemary, or even miniature olive trees. These can often be given away or planted in your yard after the event.

making it personal
More than for any other occasion, it is often for birthdays that a specific theme is used as the starting point for inspiration for the table decorations. Hobbies, favorite things, or even places are worked into the design of the party. Recreating Provençe, Greece, or Italy have been requests as well as theming children's birthdays around their favorite characters or even films. We have done Wild West parties with giant cacti through to genteel tea dances with chintz clothes and pretty heart-shaped topiary decorations on the tables. A penchant for chess involved a black-and-white theme with rose checkerboards. Winnie the Pooh has been a surprisingly popular theme for children, and those of us who would prefer to stay eternally young, there is always Peter Pan! My all-time favorite flower arrangement for a birthday table is the birthday cake design, which makes a great centerpiece with its massed thin taper candles. There is a rather grand tiered version in the anniversary section on page 160.

For female birthdays I prefer to use favorite flowers or colors to decorate parties. Seasonal flowers that are at their peak in quality and value and represent the time of year are best. For my own birthday I am fortunate to be able to use ranunculus, my favorite flowers, when they are at their seasonal best at the end of April.

For children's parties, there are so many other items to buy that the floral decoration needs to be kept to a minimum. I usually choose some of the miniature "tot" plants that are available, such as miniature

materials

a fluted stemmed glass vase

a straight-sided glass vase

a roll of tie

14 oz (400 g) sherbet disks

7 *Rosa* 'Sweet Avalanche'

7 *Rosa* 'Prima Donna'

7 *Rosa* 'Versilla'

20 *Scabiosa caucasica* 'Stäfa'

5 stems of *Hydrangea macrophylla* 'Schneeball'

7 stems of *Eustoma grandiflorum* 'Mariachi Blue'

7 stems of *Eustoma grandiflorum* 'Echo Champagne'

7 stems of green dill (*Anethum graveolens*)

10 stems of *Alchemilla mollis*

a roll of floral bind wire

sherbet surprise

Glassware is so versatile, and for birthdays and bar mitzvahs adding candy to the vase is a fairly inexpensive way of making a container that can be enjoyed after the event! The pastel colors of the sherbets provide the inspiration for an unusual color combination. For more dramatic color combinations, you could use jelly beans or M&Ms.

Step 1 Place a few sherbet disks into the bottom of the vase. Then place the straight-sided glass vase into the flared vase and fill the gap between the two with candy.

Step 2 Strip any leaves off the lower stems of the flowers and foliage. Spiral the stems into a hand-tied bouquet. This means arranging your stems at an angle in the same direction around one central stem. Twist the bunch in your hands, turning, so you work on all sides and the bunch is well balanced.

Step 3 Cut a length of floral bind wire to secure the stems and trim all the stems to the same length. Carefully fill the inner vase with water, taking care not to let any drip onto the delicate sherbet disks. Place the hand-tied arrangement in the inner vase to finish.

coming of age

If the subject of an eighteenth birthday party is a woman, I like to use simple decorations and pretty flowers. I may make eighteen small arrangements so the hostess can give eighteen of her closest friends a flower arrangement to take home. Small glasses filled with colored sand or grit can be matched to any theme. I also use lots of small terracotta pots, which are inexpensive to buy and can easily be given a lick of spray paint to suit any tone of celebration. For twenty-first celebrations I may use more sophisticated designs, but I still try to reflect the personality of the person. You can ask their best friends what flower they think reflects their persona. You'd be surprised how accurate their choices are and what that says about a person!

For male birthdays there are definitely flowers seen as more "masculine" in their feel and look. Tropical flowers with their bright colors and strong shapes are ideal. I like to mix red heliconias with anthuriums and tropical leaves or use the bright orange accent color of the strelitzia with deeper blues and purples.

There is a list of birth flowers said to be associated with birthday dates, but they seem to vary and are not particularly seasonal, so I am not sure how they came about or personally how relevant they are. According to certain charts, the dahlia flower is my birth flower. I absolutely adore dahlias, but the fact that they do not flower until the middle of the summer seems slightly at odds with my April birthday. The same can be said of my husband's so-called birth flowers. He was born in September, and for him forget-me-nots are listed, which are late spring flowers and are therefore not usually available in September! Even with worldwide transportation and the globalizing of many traditional seasonal goods, this list seems unhelpful, and I think you are better guided by personal taste and true seasonal availability at the time of the celebration.

ABOVE White and pink petals are used as a decorative device to fill tall glass vases on the welcome bar for an outdoor summer birthday party.
LEFT Pink votives and rose petals scattered over a plain white cloth decorate a side table for a simple inexpensive, but very effective decoration.
RIGHT AND OPPOSITE Tall pink vases with posies of three roses in a collar of galax leaves decorate the occasional tables. For significant birthdays such as the eighteenth and twenty-first, you can make a specific number of repeated arrangements such as these— one for each year the host is celebrating.

LEFT The glossy finish on this
black urn is matched by the
richness of the flowers and
foliage chosen to fill it: 'Black
Baccara' roses, 'Ronaldo'
tulips, and shiny black *Viburnum
tinus* berries. A 'Black Baccara'
rose tied with some viburnum
berries decorates each napkin.
RIGHT A contemporary spin on
that traditional symbol of
romance, the rose: a hand-tied
bunch of chocolate cosmos,
Zantedeschia 'Schwarzwalder,'
and 'Black Baccara' rose
encircled by green ivy trails.

romantic dining

Romance is by far the most popular reason for buying flowers. Many
partners have flowers that are significant to their relationship, and
among the other special flowers that are most often requested are
sunflowers, peonies, lilies, tulips, and, of course, orchids. Scented or
fragrant flowers are also considered very romantic. Gardenia, tuberose,
lily-of-the-valley, and freesia are often requested to make romantic
gestures or to set the mood for a dinner *à deux*!

LEFT When you are planning the floral decorations for a romantic dinner for two, it is best to avoid overly pretty or feminine arrangements. This geometric orange cube vase filled with *Brachyglottis* 'Sunshine', ivy berries, and 'Milva' and 'Renate' roses is understated yet chic.
RIGHT A huge glass globe is filled with a floral foam ball covered in 'Avalanche' roses. A sculptural shape such as this works best when the background is kept simple, so it looks great coordinated with all-white table linen.

valentine's day
In many parts of the world, Valentine's Day is one of the busiest days for the flower businesses and for romance. By far the most popular flower in the world to signify romance is the rose. On February 13 and 14, starry-eyed lovers will spend millions on flowers—and the bulk of this money will go to roses, which are still considered a token of love and affection and the universal symbol for romance. Valentine's Day has become very big business, and it has permeated the whole gift and greeting card market. However, there has not really been any decline in the demand for delivered flowers, mainly because most Valentine's Day flowers are sent anonymously. The fact that this is such a busy day for the flower industry probably has more to do with shyness and reserve than the love of romance or even flowers!

When I first began my floristry career, the best roses in the bleak cold winter month of February were those grown in the sun, primarily from South America. Rather like forced strawberries, which rarely taste as good in February, roses grown in Europe under artificial lights did not delight as much as those that had basked in true sunlight. Since those days, there are now lots of roses produced in other warmer climates such as Africa and Israel, and advances in cultivation in the Netherlands now mean that a rose grown under artificial light and heat conditions in Holland can have as large a head and strong a stem as any grown in sunnier climes.

The well-known fact about Valentine's flowers is they are usually more expensive than at other times of the year. The demand for roses and red flowers is so great that it forces the prices up. Most flowers will have come from the Netherlands or will have passed through the huge Dutch auctions—the Dutch act as flower-brokers for the world, providing well over 60 percent of all commercially sold flowers. Because demand usually exceeds supply, particularly of long-stemmed, top-quality roses, their price is forced up by as much as five times their normal cost.

Roses are normally very reliable and long-lasting flowers, but most people at some time or another have been disappointed by them when their heads flop at the neck. The reason for this is that an air lock has blocked the stem, which has meant that water from the vase cannot reach the flower head, and it flops. You can temporarily revive a rose that has drooped in this way by wrapping their heads carefully with paper and then recutting the stems with a slanted cut. Next, plunge the tips of their stems into boiling water for ten seconds. This hot-water treatment will clear any air locks in the stem. You can then rearrange the roses in clean cold water, and they will revive as new.

materials

3 blocks of floral foam

a 12-in (30-cm) straight glass bowl

15 stems of *Rosa* 'Grand Prix'

15 stems of *Rosa* 'Black Baccara'

a bunch of red dogwood

2 bunches of trailing green ivies

2 bunches of red skimmia

a bunch of *Viburnum tinus* berries

a pack of rhinestone pins

a plastic water bottle

sultry red roses

A round straight-sided glass bowl is one of the most versatile things that I use. It looks great with just a few flower heads and the odd floating candle for casual dining, but can be really dressed up for special occasions. Here, the red roses are studded with rhinestones to create a rich and romantic look.

Step 1 Place the dogwood around the bowl in a circular movement, starting from the base and working up to the rim of the bowl. Take the soaked floral foam and place and cut it so the foam is at least 2 in (5 cm) over the top of the bowl.

Step 2 Place the skimmia around the bowl with all the stems radiating from a central point. Move the bowl around so you are working on all sides and it will appear even. Add the black-berried viburnum and then place the bowl on the floor so you can see it from a greater distance. This will help make sure you are creating a round shape.

Step 3 Add the roses at different heights around the bowl. To create a very domed effect, place the flower heads at the same depth. Stud the center of the roses with the rhinestone pins. There are lots of floral accessories like this on the market, and it is very easy to find a mail-order or internet supplier. Add a few trails of green ivy across the flower heads, taking care to place the end in the foam so it stays fresh. Finally, fill with water mixed with flower food and mist the flower heads to keep them fresh.

BELOW LEFT Phalaenopsis
orchid heads decorate a napkin.
BELOW Pink and white
phalaenopsis orchids top a
silver wedding anniversary cake
created by Eric Lanlard.
RIGHT For the silver wedding
table, white tulips, phalaenopsis
orchids, ranunculus, and lilac
have been used in tall and low
frosted vases to create different
heights. Individual places are
marked with a planted
snowdrop in a silver cube and
a miniature succulent plant.

family celebrations

Increasingly, flowers are central to all family celebrations as a
way to personalize the event and very often as an extra gift to
take home after it is over to remind guests of a lovely day. It
is for this type of event that it is important to bear in mind the
container you use for your arrangement—it either needs to be
cheap enough to donate as an extra gift or perhaps if it is
expensive, it becomes part of a shared present.

LEFT A three-tiered golden wedding anniversary arrangement is topped with yellow tapers. This buffet table arrangement has been created by stacking three glass bowls on top of one another and using rings of *Viburnum opulus*, *Alchemilla mollis*, green dill, and 'Mama Mia' and 'Yellow Dot' roses.

anniversaries Celebrations to

commemorate the anniversary of a particular event, particularly a wedding, are another very popular occasion for flowers. Traditionally, there is a list of gifts that are suitable for each anniversary, and many of them provide a perfect accessory for flowers. For the first anniversary, paper is suggested, so that could easily be incorporated in the wrapping. The fifth anniversary is wood, so a lovely carved wooden bowl could make the perfect container for a central display. Iron to celebrate the sixth, tin for the tenth, steel for the eleventh are equally suitable, as are lace, ivory, and crystal for years thirteen to fifteen. The major anniversaries, twenty (china), twenty-five (silver), thirty (pearl) and forty (ruby), are all easy to interpret. And for the lucky ones among us who get to gold at fifty years and diamonds at sixty, they are also easy to decorate with flowers and/or accessories.

Whether your budget runs to a fine piece of crystal from Baccarat, a wonderful heirloom from Lalique, something stylish and architectural such as a 1930's Aalto vase from the great Finnish Modernist designer, or something cheap, practical, and cheerful from the ubiquitous household chain Ikea, my aim in creating a flower design is that the container and the flowers are in harmony. I love to make my own containers to create a sculptural look. The chosen venue will often dictate the type of container. For a small country summer celebration, I may use lavender or wheat to conceal small plastic pots. For spring, you cannot beat swirls of pussy willow lining the inside of a glass vase. Fall brings lots of fruits and vegetables to use, but American oak leaves placed around a container are perfect for evoking the season.

ABOVE A stemmed glass bowl has been edged with pearlized shells and filled with lilac, *Viburnum opulus*, and 'Mama Mia' and 'Contour' roses. Pearl-headed pins are placed throughout the arrangement.

OPPOSITE Black wrought-iron candelabra are the perfect height for low centerpieces; high enough to be seen over the top of the glasses, but not so tall the guests cannot see each other. Grapes have been wired into the bottom of these arrangements of 'Con Amore,' 'Cool Water,' 'Blue Pacific,' and 'Christian' roses, with foliage of *Heuchera* 'Plum Pudding' and *Cotinus coggygria* 'Royal Purple.'

ABOVE I like to order linen long enough to fall to the floor. Silver chairs work best with lilac linen.
RIGHT Bar and buffet tables are great for tall arrangements that act as talking points. Here, a tall stemmed vase has been filled with a huge hand-tied bouquet. The glass vase has been filled with plump rich purple berries that add color.
BELOW Napkins are trimmed with a 'Blue Pacific' rose and a striped voile ribbon.

family engagement party
For intimate family gatherings to celebrate a betrothal, a wooded garden provides a very romantic setting. Lilac and pink is my very favourite combination and one I often return to, particularly in spring and summer when the flowers available in this palette abound. This engagement dinner has been given a more sophisticated look by the addition of dark black grapes and also some very special deep foliage. The stars of these arrangements are not so much the wonderful flowers with their rich colors, but the backdrop of cotinus and heuchera. These deep wine- and eggplant-colored foliages make this combination very romantic and mysterious. In the same way that Dutch still-life painters used black backgrounds to make their vases and urns of flowers arresting, the use of dark foliage for flower arrangers produces the same result. The choice of linen is also very important for displaying the flowers to their best. For some events we choose the flowers after the linen has been chosen, but most often we discuss the flowers first and then decide which table linen will best suit our chosen combination. Here the choice of lilac accentuates the use of that color in the combination.

Nowadays, engagements are most often family celebrations and tend to be informal lunches. With the trend moving away from marriage for life and the increasing pattern of people living together, less emphasis is placed on the betrothal. The flowers for these are often simply arranged, and most popular are tied bunches.

LEFT The purity of white always seems appropriate for christening arrangements, and is, of course, suitable for both boys and girls. This all-white design of hydrangea, roses, and eustoma is set in a plain white ceramic cube.

BELOW These multicolored cubes have always rather reminded me of nursery building blocks, and so it seemed a nice idea to adapt that theme for a summer christening lunch, stacking them in different formations.

OPPOSITE A detail of the christening arrangement shows the roses, peach achillea, margarita daisies, *Alchemilla mollis,* and sprigs of unripe blackberries arranged in the tops of the cubes, the color scheme of the flowers and foliage echoing the containers.

christenings

Baby showers and baby naming ceremonies are sweet occasions for florists and flower arrangers to have some fun with flowers. The ritual of baptism is practiced by many different religions and includes Christianity, Sikhism, and branches of Islam. If you are planning a formal service, it is a perfect opportunity to decorate the religious house as well as your home. As a baptism of a child usually involves a ritual with water, either the dipping or bathing of a child, our most frequent request is to decorate the font or the receptacle holding the anointed water. For more lavish celebrations we may do one or two large arrangements and even decorations for the chairs or pews. For the feast following, we have arranged many different themes and styles of flowers. We have mossed teddy bears and rabbits to create a themed event. We have created a mini Narnia theme and even used the story of Peter Pan as our inspiration for a christening of a twin boy and girl so we could incorporate the more male theme of pirates with the more female theme of fairies. Often, childlike flowers are chosen, such as gerbera daisies in their vibrant colors, or sunflowers. For much simpler and more informal celebrations, I turn to mini plants. These are perfect and make very inexpensive table decorations. For children's parties, I am a fan of simple spring flowers such as bulbs or primroses, but there are now masses of flowers that are grown as miniatures that are perfect for table centers. I even like miniature poinsettias and kalanchoes, and I would not give house room to their full-sized relatives!

LEFT In this color-themed arrangement, blue hydrangea, blue scabious, blue echinops, and blue nigella have been mixed with white hydrangea, white dahlias, green *Alchemilla mollis*, green sedum, and some green nigella seedheads.

RIGHT A simple glass bowl was filled with fake crystals on thin aluminum wires and five pink 'Tuscani' roses.

BELOW This oversized glass teacup has a slightly *Alice in Wonderland* feel and is a fun touch for a Mother's Day lunch. It is filled with petals and mixed blown roses.

mother's day

This is the biggest day for the flower industry, and most of the world celebrates the festival on the second Sunday in May, but because of historical and religious reasons, the British Mother's Day falls on the fourth Sunday in Lent. The tradition of honoring mothers dates back to the beginning of civilization with Rhea, the Mother of the Gods, being honored in ancient Greece. In the late 1600s in England, an annual observance called "Mothering Sunday" began. The origin of this holiday was found among the upper classes, whose servants generally lived with their employers; they were given a day off to return home and honor their mothers. In the UK, they may have picked wildflowers that were plentiful at the time, such as violets, or they may have taken home a cake to celebrate the occasion.

In the US in 1908, Anna Jarvis, from Grafton, West Virginia, began a campaign to establish a national Mother's Day. Jarvis persuaded her mother's church in Grafton to celebrate Mother's Day on the anniversary of her mother's death. A memorial service was held there on May 10, 1908, and in Philadelphia the following year where Jarvis had moved. Soon, Jarvis and others began a letter-writing campaign to ministers, businessmen, and politicians in their quest to establish a national Mother's Day. They were successful. President Woodrow Wilson, in 1914, made the official announcement proclaiming Mother's Day a national observance that was to be held each year on the second Sunday in May. Now most of the countries of the world have followed suit to celebrate Mother's Day on the second Sunday in May.

materials

a plastic pot

a length of 2-in (5-cm) chicken wire

a small amount of sphagnum moss

a strong basket

2 bunches of dried lavender

a length of raffia

a large bunch of *Brachyglottis* 'Sunshine'

5 branches of flowering *Viburnum tinus*

2 bunches of *Muscari*

a bunch of *Tulipa* 'Queen of Night'

a bunch of *Tulipa* 'Valery Gergiev'

a bunch of *Narcissus* 'Cheerfulness'

10 stems of *Viburnum opulus* 'Roseum'

5 stems of hyacinth

3 stems of lilac (*Syringa vulgaris* 'Ruhm von Horstenstein')

mother's day basket

Customizing containers has long been a trademark of mine, and these round baskets are perfect for attaching dried or fresh material for a very special event. Any kind of strong woven basket will work as long as the weave is not too dense. This spring arrangement has lots of fleshy soft stems, so instead of using floral foam, I have chosen to use a bowl with water and chicken wire, which will be easier to use and help the longevity of the cut flowers.

Step 1 Place the lavender in bunches with all the heads neatly at one end and cut so that they are an identical height to the basket. Tie with raffia and attach to the basket. Continue this way all around the basket.

Step 2 Place the chicken wire in the plastic bowl so that it is really firm and snug and you can pick the whole thing up by the chicken wire. Pack the bottom of the basket with moss and place the plastic pot on top so it is packed into the basket firmly.

Step 3 Position the brachyglottis and viburnum foliage in the chicken wire to give the arrangement shape and help anchor the flowers. You need to use more foliage when using chicken wire as your mechanics than you would if using floral foam.

Step 4 Add the woody stems first, using the viburnum and the lilac all around the bowl. Keep all the stems radiating from one central point and make sure you have all the varieties at different heights and angles to give a natural look. Add the softer flowers last, and use smaller flower heads such as the muscari in groups to balance the larger-headed flowers. Fill up with water mixed with flower food.

BELOW The fruits of the harvest—bunches of wheat— inspire wonderful decorations. RIGHT This arrangement is built on a metal frame that holds four candles. 'High and Magic,' 'Tucan,' 'Marie-Claire,' and 'Orange Juice' roses are mixed with dark ligustrum berries, *Leucospermum cordifolium* 'Succession,' and the mini gerbera 'Wish' on a base of glossy camellia leaves.

halloween and thanksgiving

Halloween and Thanksgiving are two autumnal celebrations that are perfect excuses for pushing out the boat and attempting some really gorgeous yet simple table displays. At this time of year, it is the foliage that is so lovely, and there is an accumulation of seed heads, fruits, or even vegetables that can be put to imaginative and inexpensive use.

LEFT A long low autumnal table center has heavy groups of dyed orange anemones, 'Tom Pearce' chrysanthemums, 'Orange Juice' and 'Eldorado' roses, *Echinacea purpurea* seed heads, and tied bunches of dried wheat. The base is a shallow dish filled with foam and covered with ivy berries. RIGHT This metal candelabra frame has been filled with red *Skimmia japonica*, ivy berries, and *Euphorbia fulgens* 'Queen of Orange.' The lily 'Brunello' is mixed with 'Milva' and 'Orange Juice' roses.

autumn festivals

The gathering of the harvest traditionally starts a season of celebrations that have very close ties with the plant material associated with their decorations, and it is certainly true that the price of white flowers in particular is raised each year at this time in the huge European flower auctions in response to their demand for the festival of All Saint's Day on November 1. Halloween is an annual event that some believe came from the Catholic Church celebration of All Saints' Day. In Latin America, the festival is known as the Day of the Dead, and whole families visit graveyards to commune with their deceased. The night before, October 31, was All Hallows' Eve, or Halloween. The traditions of today's festival may have their origins with Celtic tribes, who by the fifth century BC came to believe that disembodied spirits who had died the previous year would come back in search of living bodies to possess for the following one.

Naturally enough, those still living did not want to be possessed, and so the tradition of placing an ember inside a hollowed-out turnip was born. The Celts originally used turnips as they were plentiful and in season, but when the early pilgrims emigrated to America, they found that the pumpkins were much more plentiful, and so these new jack-o'-lanterns were adopted. Pumpkins make great inexpensive arrangements. Cut off the top, hollow out the inside, and line them with heavy plastic film. Fill with soaked green flower foam to create an inexpensive and fun container to fill with flowers and use as a wonderful centerpiece for a Halloween supper.

Thanksgiving is an American custom that started with the English colonists who left England for a new life. They became known as Pilgrims, and they celebrated days of thanksgiving as part of their religion. The American national holiday stems from a feast held in the fall of 1621 by the Pilgrims and the Wampanoag, the American natives living in New England. This dinner to celebrate the colony's first successful harvest is still, of course, an important national holiday.

My favorite designs for Thanksgiving include cranberries. Cranberries are a unique fruit. They can grow in very special conditions and really do well in fresh water on acid peat, in what is in effect a bog. They grow on low-lying vines and are actually harvested in the water. This means they are perfect for flower arrangements because they live a long time in water without decomposing. They are harvested in and around Massachusetts, which fittingly was the area where the first pilgrims landed, but are also grown widely across the Midwest, especially in Wisconsin. The harvest of fresh cranberries usually starts in the early fall, leading up to Thanksgiving.

materials

a large pumpkin

10 mini orange dahlias

7 *Rosa canina* rosehips

10 *Photinia* 'Red Robin'

5 *Euphorbia fulgens* 'Sunstream'

5 *Viburnum tinus* berries

3 blocks of floral foam

a piece of heavy plastic wrap

a pillar candle

a green bamboo stake

a roll of floral tape

a strong knife

pumpkin parade

Pumpkins make long-lasting natural containers for floral arrangements. They are simple to create and work well for informal parties or fall dinners. At Halloween, hollowed-out pumpkins are seen everywhere, their carved faces illuminated by a candle placed inside. For an alternative less "scary" display, pumpkins make perfect natural containers for foliage, berries, and candles.

Step 1 Soak the floral foam in water until the bubbles stop rising. Meanwhile, cut the top off the pumpkin, scoop out the seeds and line it with the heavy plastic wrap.

Step 2 Pad out the bottom of the pumpkin with the soaked floral foam. Cut one block so it fits in vertically and rises above the rim of the pumpkin by at least 2 in (5 cm). It is important the foam is plentiful and fits snugly as it needs to hold the candle and lots of stems. Secure with floral tape. Cut the bamboo stake in four and tape to the bottom of the candle to make four legs.

Step 3 Secure the candle in the center of the floral foam and add the foliage around the candle. Make sure each variety of foliage is placed at different angles and heights around the arrangement to give a natural effect. Add the dahlias, also at different heights and depths, and then the euphorbia to trail over the edge.

LEFT Winter whites set the
theme for a sparkling
Christmas: ivy berries,
silver-sprayed eryngium,
ranunculus, 'Avalanche' roses,
lilac, and astilbe constructed
on a floral foam ball set on the
top of a vase with lots of
jasmine trails.
BELOW The napkin detail is
a silver-sprayed cone and a
delicate jasmine sprig.
RIGHT The long table is
decorated with one tall silver
vase filled with whites,
greens, and silver, and small
glasses filled with astilbe,
ranunculus, and hellebores.

christmas

The tradition of decorating our houses at Christmas
can be traced back to the Roman feast of Saturnalia
in honor of Saturn, god of agriculture, as well as the
Norse celebration of the winter solstice, commonly
known as Yuletide. This is undoubtedly one of the few
times when we feel we can go to town, using plants
and greenery to beautify our homes and create a
welcoming atmosphere. Many countries have their own
special traditions that are honored each year.

LEFT A plastic bowl has been surrounded with stems of *Ilex* x *meserveae* 'Blue Prince' secured on double-sided tape and tied with cord. A foam block holds glittery waxed apples, gold taper candles, and 'Black Baccara,' 'Naomi,' and 'Cherry Brandy' roses. Each setting has a miniature poinsettia, and berried holly trims the napkins.

BELOW Blue spruce was wired onto a moss frame and then four candles taped and wired onto the base. Bunches of cinnamon, eucalyptus pods, silver-sprayed cones and willow, and wired white organza ribbon were wired on the top to create a simple long-lasting winter ring.

RIGHT Low trays were filled with foam and pine, orange cotoneaster berries, brown berried hypericum, and brachyglottis. Cones and cinnamon give texture and scent, and bright green hellebores and 'Black Baccara' and 'Léonidas' roses add color. Piles of fruit, cones, and cinnamon decorate the table.

traditional christmas
For the Finns this begins with a good clean of the house, the felling of a fir tree and the making of a tied sheaf decoration of seeds and nuts to be placed in the garden for the birds. Traditionally, the tree is decorated with candy, apples, dried fruits, and candles. The festivities start with dinner on Christmas Eve, usually of dried codfish followed by suckling pig or roast ham. In Britain our current traditions were set in the Victorian era. Before Queen Victoria's reign, nobody in Britain had heard of Santa Claus, and no one had sent or received a Christmas card. The wealth and technology generated by the Victorians changed the face of Christmas forever. When Charles Dickens wrote *A Christmas Carol* in 1843, his message was for the rich to give to the poor, but it was not long before the social changes began to influence all sections of society, and by the end of the century, the Christmas stocking became popular even if it was only filled with a few nuts, an apple, and a rather more exotic orange.

As the world becomes more multicultural and multi-faithed, the traditions of this period become more varied and unique to each family. In fact, the very essence of Christmas seems to be to create your own customs and traditions. Some of these are usually taken from memories of your childhood Christmases, and although there are always new trends and colors for Christmas, there is a very strong traditional theme that prevails.

The practice of using lots of evergreen foliage with berries, dried seed heads, nuts, and spices endures. Despite new accent colors, red and white are the perennial favorites, and these two colors usually command the highest

prices at the Dutch auctions at this time of year. It is also at this time of year that many flower and foliage growers turn their attention to how they can make their products appeal to some of the more garish excesses enjoyed at Christmas, and so lots of natural products get a lick of paint or a dusting of glitzy angel dust. In Holland, many of the fruits and vegetables that have not reached supermarket standards of size are also doused in wax and glittered or highly colored. In Italy, birch twigs and bunches of ivy berries are favorites for added color from paint and glitter, and each year the list of plant materials that get the Christmas makeover increases. For my own decorations, I tend to alternate a traditional year with a more colorful and fantastical year, but I have to admit I always find it a struggle to do my own decorations when I am at my busiest fixing up my clients' homes!

materials

a low metal urn

a wire topiary cone

a bag of sphagnum moss

a bag of garden moss

2 stems of blue spruce (*Picea pungens* 'Glauca')

5 stems of variegated holly

3 stems of *Viburnum tinus* berries

3 stems of ivy berries

a selection of decorations: dried seed heads, *Plumosum* cones, cones of *Leucadendron rubrum*, star fish

a can of silver spray paint

7 limes

a selection of heavy stub wires

a spool of wire

festive topiary tree

Moss topiaries are more time-consuming than foam ones to make, but the reward is in the longevity of the design. You can use heavier plant material, which can be relatively inexpensive. They are popular in the winter when we use fruits and seed heads, adapting to the season with a dash of spray paint and glitter.

Step 1 Tease the sphagnum moss and take out any foreign bodies like bark, cones, and insects! Get some air into the matted moss and then stuff it into the center of the wire cone. Mist the moss to keep it moist. Make some hairpins from the stub wires.

Step 2 Place the cone firmly into the urn and then pass the stub wires through the base of the cone at 4 in (10 cm) intervals and hook them over the top of the edge of the urn. Then wrap the wire around the cone and secure it in the urn. The cone will be heavy when completed, so it is vital that it is well balanced and firm in the container. Place a layer of garden moss over the cone and pin in place with hairpin stub wires.

Step 3 Double leg-mount all the material by taking one heavy stub wire and bending it into two like a hairpin, then taking one side and looping it three times over the stem and the other wire so the plant material is held firm. Wire the fruit by placing a heavy wire through the flesh and twisting one wire over the other three times. Wire the fir cones by placing a wire around the base and twisting the two ends together. Spray paint any dried seed heads or accessories.

Step 4 You are now ready to place all the material in the moist moss. Start with the foliage, making sure you mix up the varieties so that there is a lovely textural effect. Add the dried seed heads and starfish, and finally the fresh limes. Mist the moss to keep the topiary fresh.

tools and techniques

Whether you grow your own flowers or buy them, the tools illustrated here will help you arrange your flowers and foliage to professional standards.

cutting tools

One of the most important pieces of equipment for a florist is a sharp cutting implement. Scissors or a knife are vital for cleanly cutting the ends off all sorts of stems. Some scissors combine a cutting blade for fresh materials and ribbon with a wire cutting area at the base. Pruners are useful for cutting hard woody stems, twigs, branches, and heavier flowers.

When cutting floral foam, a long-bladed cutting knife is very useful for giving a clean edge. Strippers can be used to quickly strip roses of their thorns and excess leaves, and wire cutters can be used to cut wire when scissors may not be strong enough.

tapes and adhesives

There are two main types of floral tape, which are used for taping wires and wedding work. One is a plastic tape, while the other is made of high-quality paper. Most florists have a preference for which one they use. Both are waterproof and come in different colors, dark green being the least conspicuous color for general use since it resembles the natural color of most stems. Taping not only conceals wires, giving the stems a natural appearance, but it is also very important in sealing stems, which prolongs the life of the plant material by slowing the dehydration process. Double-sided cellophane tape is often very useful. It can be used to cover a container, which can then be decorated with leaves, rosemary, or snakegrass. Oasis Fix is a waterproof green claylike adhesive supplied on a roll, which is used to secure pinholders and frogs in containers or onto bases.

wire products

Stub wires come in various thicknesses or gauges, starting with very fine silver wire, which is suitable for wiring the most delicate flowers and leaves, as well as individual flowerets or larger flowers for bridal work. Heavy-gauge wire is necessary for supporting large flower heads and fruits and vegetables. It is important to match the wire gauge to the plant material. The correct gauge wire is the lightest one possible that will support the material. Wires are used to control and support plant materials, reduce weight, and lengthen stems.

Florists also have a preference for the product they use to bind stems, for example, when binding a hand-tied bouquet. Bind wire, which is strong wire covered in paper, is often a popular choice.

tools and equipment

❶ small knife
❷ long-bladed cutting knife
❸ wire cutters
❹ pruners
❺ scissors
❻ stapler
❼ rose strippers
❽ ❾ ❿ stub wires (various gauges)
⓫ film tape
⓬ double-sided Cellophane tape
⓭ paper tape
⓮ Oasis Fix
⓯ lighter (for candles)
⓰ bind wire

containers and mechanics

1 When creating an arrangement using green floral foam, first soak the foam by floating it on water and letting it sink. Do not force it under. Then, place it in the container and shape accordingly. If necessary, secure with tape.

2 Pinholders are useful for securing long-stemmed flowers such as gerbera. Place a piece of Oasis Fix on the underside of the pinholder and position it in the center of the bowl. The pinholder provides a stable base for inserting stems, with the spikes securing them in place.

3 Delicate flowers and foliage are best arranged in a base of medium-gauge wire mesh, crumpled into a loose ball and placed inside the container.

4 When you wish to create a geometric shape without any visible mechanics, ordinary cellophane tape is the answer. Here, a grid of tape is added to a rectangular vase to support the flowers.

1

2

3

4

essential containers

vase selection The essential component to a well-designed flower arrangement is a great vase. For a long time the choice of vases was very limited and a lot of them were simply too decorative or their shape was too inhibitive for flowers. In the last twenty years, there has been a revolution in the choice of vases, and now so many are specifically made with flower fashions in mind. Twenty years ago, one tended to go for simple clear glass shapes that were in the main quite modest. Now that the flower trend has been for deconstructed flowers or grand party flowers, there are an enormous amount of oversized flower vases on the market in a bewildering choice of sizes and shapes.

The best place to start is by purchasing a few classic shapes that can be adapted for use throughout the year. For this reason I am still a huge fan of glass, which allows you to dress the vase up or down as the occasion may require. At its simplest, glass is lovely because you can see the natural stems of the material and view the arrangement in its entirety. If you want to make it more extravagant and special, you can add color to the water, small accessories, or fruit and vegetables. If you want the arrangement to look more sculptural, you can either use double-sided tape to affix different types of plant material or fabric on the outside or reeds, leaves, or branches to line the inside of the vase. For a very special occasion, cellophane and petals or even wire and flower heads create an arresting contemporary look.

In my own home and for the majority of arrangements, I prefer glass because it is so versatile and can be used again and again in so many ways. I love using plant material in the vase so that the whole effect is more sculptural and the vase has empathy with the flowers. The smallest in my collection are recycled French glass yogurt jars, which are perfect for small-headed delicate flowers like lily-of-the-valley and muscari, up to enormously tall yard-length glass cylinders for lilies and amaryllis. For tall vases for hall tables you need to have a vase that is at least half the height of your flowers to create a graceful design. The average length of cut flowers is 24–30 in (60–75 cm), but the best quality flowers are often around three feet long. I recommend then having a few vases around two to three feet tall for creating really grand entrance arrangements that make a statement and set the scene.

❶ Cube vase My most versatile and useful vase for over a decade. This simple shape is an essential, perfect for table centers and can be easily dressed up or down by using the inside of the vase as part of the design. Great for foam or water.

❷ Large rectangular vase Any vase which is around 6–8 in (16–20 cm) high is perfect for table flowers since you can use the vase in lots of different ways. With the flower heads cut just above the rim you have the perfect height for a table.

❸ Tall slender vase Very useful for single stems, often massed together down the center of a table to create a collection. These work well for very special flowers such as calla lilies or anthuriums, whose overall shape is architectural.

④ Trio of skinny vases
Odd numbers do work better than even when it comes to flower arranging, and a collection of three vases looks good for the center of a coffee table or a dining table when the budget is limited. Mass votives around the base to make more impact.

⑤ Tall square vase A heavy-bottomed vase is necessary for tall heavy flowers such as spires of gladioli, as seen in the picture above. A few twigs also help you to arrange the flowers, so matching red dogwood has been used here to tone with the gladioli. The reasonably thin width of the vase is just perfect for a modest collection of flowers and great for console tables.

⑥ Squat cylinder vase
A great height for dining tables and perfect for domes of roses or spring flowers. We often use leaves inside the vase to give a more natural effect, but this size is also perfect to fill with flowers and also decorative fruit and vegetables. Favourites include smaller fruits such as blueberries, crab apples, cranberries, or decorative vegetables such as chilies or small patty pan squash.

⑦ Storm lantern This shape is useful for candles as well as flowers, and I recommend a selection of these for any home. At 10 in (25 cm) they are the perfect height for most cut flowers and also

double up for candles. We use ornamental sand in the bottom to anchor the candle and help with the cleaning of the vase. For more extravagant occasions use petals with candles.

⑧ Tall elliptical vase This is the perfect vase for slim tables and for everyday flowers at home. The average home dining room table is often quite narrow and so this is perfect for dotting down the center in twos or threes depending on the length of your table. This is also a favorite size for many of our restaurant contracts. It is wide enough not to look skimpy, but not so big the quantities of flowers makes the weekly fill too expensive.

⑨ Squat elliptical vase
This vase is very popular for tables because the bottom is heavy but thin, so it is very sturdy for a few stems of flowers. It also looks elegant with just the flower heads at the top of the vase and the long length of the stem visible.

⑩ Medium cylinder vase
Cylinder vases are so versatile every serious flower arranger will have a collection of sizes. This medium-sized vase works with a mass of flower heads, as shown in the picture above, or with a group of taller flowers. It works well for hand-tied bouquets because the width allows for the spiraled stems, as the nerines demonstrate.

⑪ Small round vase This small cylinder is perfect for tight domes of flowers and is best used with twenty roses or tulips tied in a perfect round posy. I like this size as it is perfect for looking over the table, but wide enough to add accessories such as crab apples, cranberries, or chilies.

⑫ Goldfish bowl A classically shaped vase which is perfect for hand-tied bouquets because the bowl shape allows the stems to fan out and holds the spiraled stems perfectly. Also useful for floating flower heads such as blown roses or peonies and also for using one or two stems of calla lilies contained within the vase.

flower choice and care

conditioning flowers

Wherever you have sourced your flowers you will need to condition them first before arranging them. Conditioning is the professional term given to the period when the flower revives after its journey from the grower (or the garden), before it is arranged. All flowers benefit from being rested and conditioned before being arranged. The longer the journey, the more time they will require to recover. Sometimes flowers are transported in water by road or rail, so often they have spent no time out of water. However, flowers that are imported by air are generally out of water for several days, and then we condition them for a whole 24 hours before using them for a design.

To condition flowers you need to remove about an inch from the bottom of the stems with a diagonal cut, using a knife or pair of florists' scissors. The diagonal cut gives the maximum surface area for the flower to take up the water through the stem and into the flower head. Place the flowers into a scrupulously clean bucket of tepid water mixed with flower food. Tepid water carries more oxygen than really cold water so this helps revive the cut material. It is important that there is no foliage on the lower stem in the water when the flower is conditioning, since this causes bacteria to form that will shorten the life of the flowers or foliage. Therefore a lot of the lower foliage on a stem is removed at this stage.

If you are collecting flowers from your yard, the best time to do this is in the evening when the maximum reserves will be stored in the plant to be used in the hours of darkness. Place the garden plant material in a bucket with flower food overnight and it will be ready for use in the morning.

Here are some useful tips for the most popular table flower varieties.

Aconitum (picture **8** on page 189)
Also known as monkshood, this is a stunning flower. However, take great care when handling it, as the plant is highly poisonous. It is therefore advisable to use rubber gloves and dispose of any debris.

Anethum graveolens
Known more commonly as green dill, this highly aromatic flower has a huge umbelliferous head that is great as a filler for hand-tied posies and arrangements.

Anemone
Anemones should be bought in bud, and they are often packed in paper. They are heavy drinkers, so remember to refresh the vase water frequently. Anemones continue to grow once cut, so allow for this when creating mixed bouquets.

Anthurium andraeanum
Best used in hand-tied bouquets and vases and arranged in water rather than floral foam, because of their thirsty nature.

Arachnis
Known as the scorpion orchids, they are prized for their jewellike colors. They are thirsty by nature, so display them in water rather than floral foam.

Astilbe
Pretty, fluffy, and delicate, astilbe are great for summer arrangements. They can dry out very quickly, so are best arranged in water, rather than foam.

Bouvardia
Bouvardias are usually sold with special flower food and wrapped tightly to prevent limpness. The main season is from late spring to early winter, but some are available throughout the year.

Brassica oleracea
The season of the ornamental kale has been widely extended as the popularity of this long-lasting chunky headed "flower" has continued to grow.

Callicarpa bodinieri
Excellent for vase arrangements and great for autumn weddings. The short season of this plant makes it an annual treat, and the extraordinary color of the berries is often a talking point.

Campanula medium
Excellent for summer vases and large arrangements. The multi-headed stem survives better in water than in foam and should never be allowed to dry out.

Celosia
The rich vivid colors of celosia and their unusual texture add uniqueness in hand-tieds bouquets and arrangements of any size. Place in a clean vase with cut-flower food. Avoid fluctuations in temperature if you want a long-lasting display.

Chrysanthemum (picture **3** on page 189)
Chrysanthemums are extremely versatile and long lasting. Their vase life is generally from seven to ten days, though some varieties will last as long as three weeks if you change the water regurlarly.

Cymbidium
Good for weddings and corporate work and—because they are extravagant and symbolize love—popular for Valentine's Day. Also, a good long-lasting cut flower for the holiday season.

Dahlia
Dahlias are the most gorgeous members of the daisy family, available from mid-spring through to early winter, with supply peaking really between midsummer and fall.

Delphinium
The smaller varieties are great for large hand-tieds and vases, while the hybrids are excellent for large arrangements and bridal work. The addition of flower food in the water will help prevent the distinctive colors from fading and petals dropping.

Dianthus
Dianthus are suitable for all aspects of floristry and flower arranging, but are particularly popular sold in bunches for home decoration.

Echinops
Globe thistles make excellent cut flowers and also dry well, so are an excellent flower for more permanent arrangements. They are extremely long lasting and work well in hand-tieds and arrangements.

Eryngium
Great for flower arrangements and also for bridal work. Their vase life can range anywhere between twelve and sixteen days, sometimes longer if they are kept in cool conditions.

Eucharis
After a while the stems of eucharis become blocked and no longer take up sufficient water, so cut a piece off the stems every five days. Remove any older flowers to encourage all the buds—generally three to six—to open.

Eustoma
Available in single and double varieties, they are great for vases, hand-tied bouquets, and wedding work. Eustomas do not like light humidity, so avoid placing them in bright sunlight, where they may be prone to botrytis.

Freesia (picture **6** opposite)
Popular due to its beautiful scent. When buying, check for maturity—the main bud must be fully grown and showing colour. Never leave without water, as freesias are very sensitive to dehydration.

Gerbera
Useful for all aspects of flower arranging and floristry. Try to avoid touching the flower heads, which are easily damaged, and, as gerberas are particularly sensitive to bacteria, make sure that the vase and water are absolutely clean.

Gladiolus (picture **7** opposite)
Sometimes known as the sword lily, the gladioli is a member of the iris family. Perfect for vase arrangements, it is advisable to cut off the top bud to encourage the lower buds to open.

Gloriosa
Short-stemmed gloriosa are useful for small arrangements, while the longer trailing stems are great in bouquets and larger displays. This fragile specimen is often shipped in air-inflated plastic bags to avoid damage to the flower.

Helianthus
Sunflowers are best displayed on their own in a vase or larger arrangements. Small varieties work well in hand-tieds, although they drink a lot of water.

Heliconia
Also known as wild plantain or lobster claw, heliconias are useful for contract work and the hanging varieties are great for large decorations. They have an excellent vase life and can last up to three to four weeks.

Hermodactylus tuberosus
Also know as the widow iris, this early spring iris appears just after snowdrops and is a rare treat for Valentine's Day bouquets. It works in foam for special events, but lasts longer in water.

Hippeastrum
Amaryllis are highly valued as cut flowers because of their impressive vase life. To ensure optimum blooming, remove pollen-bearing stamens and place a bamboo cane into their hollow stem to bear the weight of the flower heads.

Hydrangea
Good for all bouquets, flower arrangements, and wedding bouquets. Remove most of the foliage to give the flower head the best chance of a long and healthy vase life.

Iris (picture **2** opposite)
Useful for flower arrangements and they make an interesting flower for vegetative or natural designs. Blue, yellow, and white varieties are available.

Lathyrus
Good for simple vase arrangements and a popular choice for weddings because of their delicacy. Sweet peas are very fragrant, and their vase life can range from eight to ten days.

Leucospermum
Very useful for hand-tieds and arrangements, these flowers are excellent for contract work because of their longevity in water and florist's foam.

Lilium
Lilies are long lasting and adored for their scent. It is advisable to remove the anthers to prevent pollen staining the flowers, surfaces, or clothing.

Muscari (picture **4** opposite)
This delicate bulb flower is perfect for small table arrangements and posies. Sold in bunches, since you need quite a lot to make an impact. Make sure the bottom flowers are open when you pick or purchase this flower.

Narcissus
Great for vase arrangements and in small posies and hand-tied bouquets. The stems give off slime, which has an unfavorable effect on other flowers.

Oncidium
Great for vases and arrangements. The longevity of this striking flower makes it a staple for contract work. Mostly available in shades of yellow and brown, though it also comes in other colors, such as green, red, and magenta.

Ornithogalum
Also known as the Star of Bethlehem, they are great for arrangements, although they continue to grow when they are cut, so make sure you leave room to accommodate this new growth.

Paeonia
Peonies are prized for all kinds of floristry and flower arranging. They are also extremely popular for summer weddings and depending on the variety, range from slightly fragrant to heavily scented.

Papaver
Poppies are very popular as cut flowers; sadly, however, they are short-lived. Most are supplied with their stems singed because they exude a milky sap. If you need to trim them, ensure that you re-singe them in a naked flame.

Paphiopedilum
Also known as slipper orchid, these long-lasting blooms are expensive and so their use tends to be restricted to specialized floristry for wedding and high-design work. They have hairy stems that do not like being in deep water, so place them in very shallow water.

Phalaenopsis
Good for wedding bouquets, displaying in single vases, and in decorative floristry, these orchids are excellent as pot plants. Flaccid flowers can be refreshed by submerging them in lukewarm water.

Physalis (picture **1** opposite)
Popular for autumn arrangements, particularly for Halloween. The orange lanterns can also make very cheerful dried flowers and can last for up to two years.

Protea
Protea add color, texture, and a distinctive architectural quality to floral arrangements. Do not pack flowers too tightly in buckets, as leaf blackening can be a problem with proteas. This is caused by the considerable heat that the flowers themselves generate.

Ranunculus (picture **9** opposite)
Popular in bouquets, bridal work, and arrangements. These beautiful flowers look their best the day before they expire, when their petals become translucent. Remove any lower foliage from the stems, as they will contaminate the water, before you use them.

Rosa
The most popular flower in the industry, due to its wide variation in color and size. Vase life is generally from eight to eighteen days, depending on the temperature and cultivar.

Stephanotis floribunda
Prized by florists, notably for its glorious scent, it is popular with brides all over the world. The flowers are usually sold in bags or small boxes without any greenery, so if you want to use the green tendrils and vines, you will need to specially order the plant form.

Strelitzia (picture **5** opposite)
A wonderfully exotic flower, the strelitzia is more commonly known as the bird of paradise, due to its resemblance to the beautiful bird. It is widely used in floristry due to its strong stem, long-lasting flowers and versatile nature.

Trachelium
Available all year round in lilac, purple, white, and pink. The white variety help arrangements appear fresher; however take care when you select them as they can mark if they get damp in transit.

Tulipa
Good for hand-tied bouquets and vases. Remember when creating designs, that the tulips will continue to grow in water, sometimes as much as 2in (5cm).

Vanda
Perfect for boutonnieres, corsages, and exotic arrangements. Vanda orchids are expensive to buy, but will last up to an impressive three weeks in water and so give excellent value.

Zantedeschia
Known as the calla or arum lily, these are very versatile flowers, which are useful for all aspects of flower arranging. You can protect the stems from splitting by taping the ends with clear tape.

❶ ❷ ❸ ❹ ❺ ❻ ❼ ❽ ❾

index

acknowledgments

A very strong female team has put this book together! At the top, my Publisher Jacqui Small whose commitment to creating a book is legendary both in the end results and the process—thank you for assembling an exceptionally devoted and hard-working team. A huge thanks to the photographer Sarah Cuttle for her sensitive and beautiful images, and for so cheerfully working hard on this project. Thank you to her assistants for all their enthusiasm and help. My wonderful Art Editor Maggie Town has kept me from straying too far from the flat plan and created a very visually stunning book. A very long suffering Sian Parkhouse, who is my lovely editor, exerted just the right kind of pressure and made very positive noises at exactly the right time.

To my experienced and wonderful team, headed up by the extremely talented Sarah Jackson who never seems to let the pressure faze her and who has the amazing attribute of always being able to see the bright side of any situation, aided by the artistic, capable, and very chatty Samantha Griffiths. For Jo Rouse for all her input, support, and help with some of the designs. Thanks also to Penny Mallinson, Tania Newman, and Gina Jay. Thank you to all those who directly worked on this project such as Natasha Tshoukas, Annabel Murray, Ann Pochetty, Rona Wheeldon, and our students at The Flower House. Huge thanks also to my long-standing and very creative designers Chris Sharples and Anna Hudson who run London's best flower shop outside Liberty in Great Marlborough Street, London. Thank you to all the rest of my great team: Anne Cadle for her support and all the early mornings. Thanks to Anita Kovacevic for flying the flag for us in Brompton Cross and to all the rest of the team who have worked with us while this project has been on the table—Without your support I would not be able to escape to do these books! Thanks to the rest of the team: Catherine Anderton, Katie Cochrane, Kirsten Dalgleish, Yolande Davis, Belinda Ferrari, Jason Fielding, Gerry Gildea, Alison Grimley, Takuya Hirai, Shontelle Jepson, Kyoung Joo Choi, Miranda Laraso, Tammey Lea White, Hyunah Lee, Rosanna Manfredi, Victoria Nelson, Sonya Pollitt, Sarah Price, Marianne Schmidt, Richard Stavrou, Young Un Kwon, Hisako Watanabe, Jason Watson, Samantha Wilkes, Su Yeon Lee, Monika Zimmer.

Plus special thanks to all the following people:

An enormous thanks to Eric Lanlard from Savoir Design for the scrumptious cakes and also the hire of his lovely home.

To the fantastic staff at Ickworth House for all their help with our shoot there

To Terry Jones from Jones Hire for providing practically everything we needed throughout the book and also for decorating so many of our parties and weddings in London and the South East.
See their website www.joneshire.co.uk

To Jo and Ben Robins for the use of their lovely barn in Denham, a perfect venue for a country party and wedding in Suffolk.

For Beryl and John Aldous for the use of their lovely garden.

To Jenny and Phil for the use of their garden.

To the Dalham Hall Estate for location help.

Sue Maddix of Foxglove Events.

For all the people whose wedding and party flowers appear in this book:

Jenny and Martin at Westley Waterless

Nathaly and Doug at Dalham

Liz and Nick at Syon Park

Raaid and Farrah at the Dorchester Hotel

Rebecca and Amit at Waddesdon Manor

Mary and Anthony at the Penthouse at the Dorchester Hotel

Sarah and Duncan at Ashridge